Be Your Own
Home Decorator

Be Your Own Home Decorator

Creating the look you love without spending a fortune

Pauline B. Guntlow

A Storey Publishing Book

Storey Communications, Inc.

The mission of Storey Communications is to serve our customers by publishing practical information that encourages personal independence in harmony with the environment.

Edited by Deborah L. Balmuth
Photography by Kevin Kennefick (except where otherwise noted)
Line drawings by Brigita Fuhrmann
Design and production by Meredith Maker
Production assistance by Erin Lincourt
Indexed by Barbara E. Cohen

Thanks to Country Curtains, Lee, Massachusetts for photos on pages 36, 85, 89; and to Pergo Flooring for photo on page 52.

Storey Publishing books are available for special premium and promotional uses and for customized editions. For further information, please call the Custom Publishing Department at 1-800-793-9396.

Printed in Canada by Interglobe, Inc.
10 9 8 7 6 5 4 3

Library of Congress Cataloging-in-Publication Data

Guntlow, Pauline B., 1938–
    Be your own home decorator : creating the look you love without spending a fortune
/ Pauline B. Guntlow
        p.   cm.
    "A Storey Publishing Book"
    Includes bibliographical references and index.

    1. House furnishings.   2. Interior decoration—Amateurs' manuals. I. Title.
TX311.G86 1996
645—dc20

96-30158
CIP

Acknowledgments

Much appreciation to my daughter Vicky for her help with the word processing of the manuscript; to my twin brother, Paul, who made me promise to mention him in this book; and, principally, to Rich, who patiently and warmly supports me in all my projects with his encouragement and physical labor.

Contents

Introduction

Home is where we spend a good part of our leisure time. How our homes look inside helps shape our satisfaction with the time we spend there. Think about it: If you're in an environment that you don't find pleasing to look at or that functions inefficiently, you are less likely to spend much time there or to enjoy being there.

At age eighteen I rented my first apartment and discovered the joy of transforming ordinary, characterless rooms into an attractive and delightful place to live. I liked doing it so much I wasn't happy stopping at just one. I've redecorated approximately fourteen houses in the course of my career and developed some techniques for easy, relatively inexpensive things you can do to transform the look and feel of your home and make it more pleasurable for everyone living there. I'm pleased to have this chance to share these ideas with you.

What Qualifies as "Decorating"?

By my definition, decorating involves finding a look that combines personal taste and function, that satisfies your aesthetic sense as well as your practical needs. Whatever it takes to achieve that look qualifies as decorating. Some people make a distinction between decorating and remodeling, but to me they go hand in hand. Installing architectural moldings, wood floors, and tile are all part of decorating a home. I believe that the design of new construction can be part of your decorating statement. Decorating is more than moving furniture, choosing colors, and hanging curtains, although these are all part of it.

In short, you can do as little or as much as you like under the guise of decorating. In this book I offer a full range of tips and instructions, from simple no-sew curtains and 15-minute paint jobs to furniture renovation and restoration and more complex woodworking, tiling, and building projects that you can do yourself, or hire someone else to do. I'll tell you and show you how I did it, and you can take it from there. With a little inspiration from me and a little perspiration from you, you'll be amazed at the transformations you can bring about in your living space. It's a lot of fun to think about the possibilities — and even more fun to make them happen!

To identify your personal decorating style, find examples of looks you like in home decorating magazines.

Where to Begin
The Five Basic Steps of Decorating

Where do I start? Thinking about all your decorating options can be overwhelming. I've found that it helps to take a step-by-step approach, beginning with a little homework and analysis before taking any action. Here are five basic steps I find helpful to follow.

Step 1: Decide What Look You Want to Achieve

Deciding on a look or style is tough for a lot of people. There are so many wonderful possibilities. You walk into a furniture store and the array of styles is overwhelming. Then you visit a friend's home and your preferences are completely swayed by his or her style. While thumbing through a home decorating magazine you find a picture of the perfect family room.

The reality is that most of us live on budgets that limit us to working with what we've already got rather than going out and simply buying a completely new look. But you'll be surprised by how much you can change a room just by using your furnishings in different ways.

Whatever your means, deciding on the look you like is basic to decorating. No one can tell you what that is — it's your call.

COLLECT EXAMPLES OF LOOKS YOU LIKE

How do you find *your* look? A great way to start is by looking through magazines and visiting furniture stores, decorator homes, model homes, and any other places that display decorating styles. When I decided to do a Shaker-style kitchen in my house (see photo on page 44), I visited the Hancock Shaker Village in Hancock, Massachusetts, one of the best surviving examples of an authentic Shaker village. There I bought a book with many photos of Shaker buildings and furnishings. Armed with the book and my own visual observations, I designed the details that would give my kitchen a more authentic Shaker look.

Make your design research a part of your daily routine. Every week, when purchasing groceries, invest in one decorating magazine. There are magazines for almost every look and style, from *Country Living* to *Victorian Decorating* to *Architectural Digest*. Cut out pictures that appeal to you and keep them in a scrapbook. Do this for a couple of months. Then organize the pictures according to what room they illustrate. When you have at least five examples for each room of the house, analyze the pictures to determine what common denominator makes them appealing to you. Look for similar patterns — features you always like — and try to identify the look emerging from your selections. For example, you may discover that you prefer:

- Certain color families
- The unadorned, uncluttered look
- The rustic country look
- Glass and chrome, complemented by contemporary art
- Lots of wicker and Waverly prints
- Victorian velvet and tapestry

These are just a few of the many distinct styles and looks. Not having a specific style counts, too, as a look unto itself. Drawing on elements from various styles and sources qualifies as the "eclectic" look. As long as you have common color themes throughout, you can pull this look together. Some of the best rooms I've ever seen have been eclectically decorated.

If a specific style or look overwhelmingly appeals to you, you're among the lucky few. When I was twenty-one, I moved from San Diego, California, to Plattsburg, New York, where I visited a historical house filled with antiques. The look of the furnishings and architecture struck me like a bolt of lightning. I knew right then that this was the style I loved, and I have never changed my mind. Unfortunately, bolts of lightning won't strike most people. You'll have to allow time to explore different styles and live with the options for a while before deciding what direction to take in decorating your home.

FURNISHINGS AND ACCESSORIES TO FIT YOUR STYLE

One of the most important steps in achieving a particular look is to identify the furnishings and accessories that express that look and then focus on acquiring them. Here are some lists to help you get started.

Country

crocks
wooden boxes
yellow ware
primitive paintings
old toys
quilts
needlework
wooden ware
utensils with painted
   handles
spinning wheel
coffee grinders
pitcher and bowl
braided rugs
rag rugs
marbles
tinware
cookie cutters
candy and butter molds
wooden ice chest
copper washtubs
pie safes with tin inserts

Traditional

Impressionist-style
   paintings
marble busts
large paintings
grand piano
Chinese design on wall-
   to-wall sofa with fringe
   edging
black lacquered armoire
Empire chairs
gentleman's flat-top desk
hunt table behind sofa
tassels on drapes
pier mirror

Victorian

stenciled trays
paintings on velvet
mirrors in fancy gold
   frames
school clock
silver
Oriental rugs
brass beds
decorative screens
Bible
Hoosier cabinet
velvet drapes
wallpaper/borders
fans
Gone with the Wind
   lamps
Empire chests
use ribbon to hang
   pictures
damask
player pianos
piano scarf

Contemporary

glass tables
mirrored walls
lacquered furniture
modern art
wall-mounted cooking
   hood
indirect lighting
tubular metal chairs
CDs in open cupboard
bed low to floor
built-in buffet
black-and-white or
   primary colors
marbleized pillars for
   dividers

Southwestern

horse paraphernalia
   (harnesses, etc.)
boots
Mexican blankets
cow horns
crocks
leather
natural-colored wicker
iron lamps
terracotta planters
cactus
trunks
sombreros
plaster-finish walls

Colonial

Oriental rugs
Queen Anne furniture
grandfather clock
Chippendale furniture
candle stands
highboys
hatboxes
tester beds
six-board chests
settles
wash benches
Chinese porcelains
ladder-back chairs
stepback cupboards
pewter
window seats
candlesticks
corner cupboard
paintings in gilt frames
pole screen

Craftsman/Mission

Art Deco lamps
silk scarves
tables decorated with tile
Tiffany glass
oak side chairs with leather-
   covered seats
carnival glass
bronze statuary
mission furniture
stained glass
what-not shelf
Victrola

French Provincial

side chairs with curved legs
   and gold striping
damask and silk fabric
heavy, painted ceiling moldings combined with elon-
   gated wall moldings in
   paneled design
parquet floors
quilt frames
screens with painted designs
marble
tapestries
porcelain dishes on walls
dish racks
small painted porcelain
   boxes
prismed chandeliers
grandfather clock
   (marquetry)
sterling silver
breakfront bookcases
crewelwork
heavy ball fringe on drapes
fainting sofa
pier mirrors
sconces

IDENTIFY KEY ELEMENTS OF THE LOOK YOU LIKE

Once you've narrowed in on the look you like, you can begin to identify specific features that you would want to duplicate in your house. Go back to your scrapbook and scrutinize the pictures you collected. What kind of furniture do you see? What are the window treatments? How are the floors treated? For example, if your taste runs more to the traditional look, you might note that four out of the five living room pictures you picked show floor-length drapes. This is key to achieving the look you like. You may then realize that what you have now are curtains that come to just below the window casing. Therefore, creating new window treatments is going to be on your list. Apply the same analysis to furniture, fabric, and accessories, and write down your choices as you work.

Each decorating style is associated with particular furnishings and accent accessories that enhance the overall theme. For example, Tiffany hanging lamps are identified with the Victorian look, while glass and metal coffee tables are decidedly contemporary. But many styles overlap. Treasured pieces of furniture that have been preserved and passed down from one generation to the next become part of a new look.

New designs in furniture are often slow to catch on. Trends that start in one city or country may take years to become popular in small, out-of-the-way towns. That is one reason overlapping furniture styles and accessories are

This eclectic group of bedroom furnishings includes a 1920s chest (at left), an 18th century oak cupboard, and miscellaneous smalls.

EXAMPLE OF AN ECLECTIC LOOK

An eclectic look includes furnishings and accents from a variety of styles. For example, the following elements in a living room include one homeowner's favorite belongings:

- China-white walls
- Glass-top coffee table
- Wingback sofa in tan and brown print with a touch of mustard
- Pair of contemporary mustard-colored recliners
- Maple desk
- Mustard and china-white striped drapes
- Tan sisal carpet
- Collection of various-size brass pots with plants
- Mirrors with antique gold frames

The eclectic combination works because even though furniture styles and wood colors are mixed, there are common colors and patterns running throughout the room. Moreover, the accessories, such as the brass pots and gold-framed mirrors, do a lot to pull the room together.

fairly common. Well-defined lines between furniture styles are rare. This means that achieving a particular style allows you a great deal of flexibility; you can accommodate a variety of styles of furnishings and accessories and still achieve an identifiable look. Any restrictions in decorating styles are imposed by you and you alone.

TRUST YOUR DECISIONS

Once you've spent all this time researching, analyzing, and making choices about the look you like, trust the decisions you've made. I don't want to sound tyrannical, but if you arc living with a mate who cares little about how the house is decorated, trust your own judgment for the final choice. Don't allow last-minute input from someone who hasn't been part of the process of analyzing and selecting to influence your decisions. For instance, if you've spent hours deliberating on a color choice between two close shades of off-white and feel confident about the decision, don't let someone else come along and contradict you after just two minutes of consideration. (The exception to this is a person with very good color sense.) Trust your instincts.

The spacious-feeling, contemporary design of this house is complemented by the colored walls and light-colored sofa.

Step 2: Select a Color Scheme

The ability to use color effectively in fabrics, on walls, furniture, and flooring is critical to successful decorating. "Color" is probably the most frequently used word in this book, because it is *the most important factor* in decorating. You can have the most exquisite furnishings that, taken individually, are beautiful; collectively, however, if the colors don't work well together, you might as well have orange crates for furniture.

You may be among the many people who doubt their ability to put colors together, or you may feel you don't have enough money to color-coordinate your furnishings. Neither an art degree nor a fortune is required to develop

To focus in on your taste in colors, ask yourself the following questions:

What rooms am I decorating?

How much light comes in the windows of each room?

What background colors do I like — for the walls, floors, carpeting?

What colors do I like in large amounts, as accents?

What pieces of upholstered or painted furniture do I have to work with, and what color are they?

Being specific in your answers will help you concentrate on your goal.

successful color schemes. You can put one together with some basic knowledge and a minimum investment. A great color scheme doesn't cost any more than a terrible one.

PERFORMING A COLOR INVENTORY

To develop a color scheme for your home, I suggest a step-by-step approach similar to that described above for determining style. To begin, look around your house, room by room, and assess by color the significant factors (furniture, walls, floors, and so on) within each room. Scrutinize each item closely to decide whether it is worth keeping, could be renovated, or needs to be replaced. This will give you an inventory of the colors you're starting with. For each element in the room, determine and write down how it meets the following criteria.

Color. Are there any colors in the room that you immediately react to, positively or negatively? Is the carpet a color you really dislike? Do not be concerned about pieces that are exclusively wood-toned, such as a mahogany coffee table. Wood tones will blend into just about any color scheme, including other wood tones.

Can the color be changed by fabric or paint?

Can the piece of furniture be moved to another room to fit into a different color scheme?

Although not dealing with color directly, ask yourself the following three questions regarding general assessment. The answers will further clarify your color inventory.

Condition. Is it fairly new? Does it need significant repairs? Do the walls need to be repainted? If it's a piece of furniture, does it need to be slipcovered or upholstered?

Usefulness. Should you remove the piano if it is no longer used? Is the entertainment center too small to accommodate all your tapes? There are too many side chairs in the living room; should you remove some?

Size. Is the sofa too big or too small for the room? Is the bed cumbersome looking in this room?

Once you've done this initial written assessment, gather color samples of everything in each room. Snip small pieces of fabric from the underside of chairs or the inside of slipcovers. In the case of items from which you can't remove a small sample (such as carpet and walls), get color chips from a paint store that match your wall and floor colors. Put all these samples in a folder.

Now bring out that scrapbook you put together for determining your style (see page 2) and take another look at the pictures of decorated rooms. Note the predominant colors in the style you selected. Think of ways you can incorporate the elements in your room that you don't want to change into the new color scheme. A few simple techniques will help you figure out how to combine colors.

Negotiating Color Choices with Others in Your Household

A fairly common color-choice dilemma is presented when you and your partner like different colors. But don't despair. Even if one of you is adamant about using a particular color, a color scheme can usually be worked out to include tones that both of you can live with.

For example, you find a great sofa on sale in a dark bottle-green print. You like the sofa and know it's a tremendous buy. Your partner is not happy with the color and thinks it will make the living room too dark. The sofa has tiny specks of gold and blue in it. Gold as an accent color is acceptable to your partner, but you would prefer blue. Gold is on the bright side of the color wheel and will make the room look sunnier. Use the gold in at least one chair and the drapes: it will brighten the room tremendously. Show your partner how the introduction of gold will eliminate the issue of the living room appearing dark. Use blue for smaller accessories such as throw pillows.

If your situation is more drastic — you're negotiating with a person who can only imagine the living room decorated completely in brown (a color you detest) — your strategy should be slightly different. Stay away from a my-color-choice-is-better-than-yours discussion. Instead present a well-thought-out color plan complete with color chips and fabric samples. Extend the conversation over several weeks. Find examples in magazines of color schemes that include not only brown but also accent colors you could live with. You might say something like, "Oh, look, there's a brown leather chair in the shade you like." From there you slide into, "Oh, and they've put a blue sofa with it. Do you think that's a nice combination?" You could even say, "You know, you're right about a brown chair."

The idea here is not to tell housemates they are completely wrong in all their color suggestions (even if they have rotten taste). Give them a chance to back down, or negotiate gracefully by agreeing with part of what they say. Ask questions like, "Do you suppose . . ." or "How do you think that will work?" Say, "I placed a towel on the chair in the same shade we're thinking of doing it over in so we can see how we feel about it in a few days." I know, this sounds like the radio psychologist Dr. Lora Schlesinger dealing with a family crisis. Meshing two people's tastes may not be a crisis exactly, but it *is* a challenge.

Borrowing Color Schemes from Nature

One of the most popular color schemes is blue and white. Sky blue and snow white — you can't miss when you copy Mother Nature. There is nothing more beautiful than blue sky, deep green moss, yellow marigolds, and autumn leaves.

Color schemes can be taken from the sea, too: the tones of the sand and the various shades of gray-green to blue-green of the water.

Natural Color Combinations

Colors from nature can be combined in a room in a number of ways. All the seasons feature superb color combinations. Sunrises and sunsets are exquisite. Here are a few examples.

Combination #1

Walls — natural patina (or stained) of pinewood paneling
Carpet — deep moss-green
Sofa and drapes — blue and green print
Accents — small chair and pillows in marigold yellow and blue

Combination #2

Walls — gray green
Carpet — dark pine flooring with brick-red Oriental rug
Sofa — gold
Drapes — brick-red print with gold and gray-green accents
Accents — gold chairs and a collection of brass candlesticks

Combination #3

Woodwork — Wedgewood blue
Walls — off-white (slightly gray tone)
Floor — wood with cherry-red finish
Sofa — yellow, red, or blue-green, or a print with those colors
Drapes — Wedgewood blue in a pattern design
Accents — coordinated with sofa color

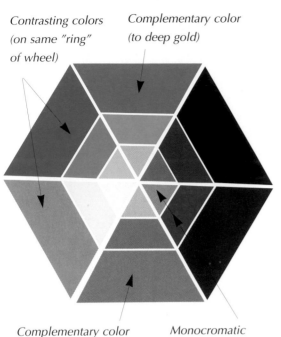

Contrasting colors (on same "ring" of wheel)

Complementary color (to deep gold)

Complementary color (to teal)

Monocromatic colors (shades of the same color)

A color wheel is an indispensible tool for planning your color scheme.

COLOR VOCABULARY

Primary (basic) colors: Blue, red, and yellow. All other colors are made up of at least two of these three.

Secondary colors: Derived from a mixture of any two primary colors. For example, red and yellow produce orange.

White and black produce neutral tones in varying shades of gray.

Neutral colors also include browns, beiges, creams, and off-whites.

USING A COLOR WHEEL

A color wheel is to decorating what a road map is to traveling — it guides you in the right direction toward pleasing, color-coordinated rooms. With a color wheel, you can quickly identify relationships between different colors, including:

Contrasting colors: Extremes within the same hue (such as pink and red)

Complementary colors: Opposite each other on the wheel (such as red and green)

Monochromatic colors: Within the same range (such as various shades of blue)

You can use the color wheel to determine what intensity of tone to use. For example, you may have a deep teal-blue sofa and wonder what com plementary shade to use on a chair in the same room. By referring to the color wheel, you'll find that deep gold is directly opposite teal, positioned in the same area of the outer ring. This is the most suitable complementary color for the chair.

Using this color wheel process, you can develop a color decorating plan for each room that you want to improve or change. Sometimes you may feel like changing a successful decorating scheme simply because you're tired of the old look. Even small changes, such as adding new throw pillows, can lift your spirits and make the room feel like a new place. For days after I change something, I sneak back, take a peek, and marvel over the difference.

When you go shopping for fabric, furniture, or other accessories, be sure to take color samples with you. It is the rare person who can remember an exact shade of a particular color. And when you select one piece of the design, go back to the color wheel and see what shades and accents will create a compatible color combination. You may not have thought of every possibility. Keep in mind that various shades of one color can blend in an interesting way. Remember, if you are not positive about the introduction of a specific color, get a sample first and try it.

Using color well is an art form. It takes thought, planning, and perhaps a bit of daring. An artist focuses on the desired effect and paints the canvas accordingly. As a home decorator, you decide on the look you want to achieve and decorate your home in keeping with that vision.

It's quite natural to ask, How do you pick a color scheme if you are starting from scratch? You may feel like a kid in a candy store trying to decide what goody to buy. If you are able to eliminate some colors from consideration right away, that's helpful. But if you have no parameters to follow, the process can be overwhelming — so many choices! The best way to start is lay out all the color options and decide which colors you immediately love and which ones you immediately dislike. Once you've removed those colors, consider the choices anew, picking your second-best favorites and eliminating your second-most disliked. Work from both ends until there are only a few contenders left.

CASE STUDY: DEVELOPING A COLOR PLAN FOR A LIVING ROOM

Consider the classic problem in sticking with a color scheme. You want to redo your living room, but you have a meager budget and don't know what to do with that homely yellow-and-black plaid sofa Aunt Mary gave you (still in good condition) and the horrible overstuffed chair.

The best tactic when you encounter established parameters — such as the yellow-and-black-plaid sofa that you can't afford to replace — is to build your color scheme around them. Don't decorate for what will be; decorate for now, because "as soon as I can afford it" has a way of stretching further and further into the future. Meanwhile, during those months and years you have to wait, you must live with decorating that does not work.

So unless you're sure you can purchase some new item within the next six months, decorate for what you have to live with now. You can add that new piece later if you plan properly.

There are two elements that are expensive and may therefore dictate color schemes: upholstered furniture and carpeting. Less costly items such as wall paint, drapes or curtains, throw pillows, and painted furniture are more easily

Color is one of the key elements tying together the furnishings, floor, walls, and accessories in this Colonial-style living room.

Finding a Color Scheme That Works

Problem: You have an off-white sofa with light blue and rose-pink splotches in it. The carpet is off-white. You want the room to feel cozy. What do you do?

Solution: Paint the walls in the shade of blue that appears in the sofa, or use wallpaper with the same blue tones. For window treatments try a fabric that's blue, solid pink, or has a pattern or stripe that repeats the sofa colors (echoing the off-white background) or put up bamboo shades with wooden valances.

A decent color scheme can be created around any one item you already own. Say your most valued piece — a Victorian love seat upholstered in plum velvet — does not match or blend with anything else in your living room. In this instance, the other items are two tan overstuffed chairs. You can test possible color schemes by going to a fabric store and looking for a design that combines the plum and tan colors in one fabric. If you have difficulty finding a workable color combination, ask for input from people whose color sense you admire.

changed. One way to change the color of an upholstered piece is to use a slipcover. Slipcovers are attractive, but unless they are made of iron-strong cloth (e.g., blue denim), they don't hold up under heavy use. If you want to put a slipcover on a sofa that is used a lot, look for a highly durable fabric in a color that won't show soiling.

Let's get back to the yellow-and-black-plaid sofa. How do you make it work? Assume your living room is 12′ by 14′ with three windows of average size, and the room includes:

- Brick fireplace with a mantel
- Yellow-and-black-plaid sofa
- Purple-and-gray floral overstuffed chair in poor condition
- Maple rocking chair
- Two small side tables
- Nondescript bookcase
- Walls painted light green
- Floor of oak hardwood

What can you do on a tight budget to bring this living room together? There are many possible color combinations. If you use the right colors, that yellow-and-black-plaid sofa will blend into your overall scheme, and Aunt Mary will love you forever because you appreciate her good taste. If you like the country look, here's one possible solution: Paint the walls, make or buy tab curtains, re-cover the upholstered chair, and buy a braided rug. This combo is definitely country.

But let's change the look to contemporary. Finding the right fabric with which to cover the purple-and-gray floral upholstered chair is the key to resolving this color dilemma. It should be a print that repeats the yellow and black of the sofa. If it has a fairly neutral background color that could also be used on the walls, such as pale yellow or medium cream, so much the better. A gold-and-black stripe would certainly work, too, although you're unlikely to find one easily. To complete the room, I'd suggest the following items: Yellow and black plaid sofa, glass and brass coffee table, very soft gold walls, black leather chair (reupholster the overstuffed one), cream-and-black-stripe tablecloth on round table with glass top (sew strips of black ribbon to cream-colored fabric), carpet in multi-fleck charcoal, gold, and cream; vertical blinds in cream, and accent throw pillows in vivid shades of primary colors in silk fabric with cording.

Here are my recommendations for a color plan for this living room:

Sofa — Keep as is in yellow-and-black plaid.

Upholstered chair — Have slipcover made in a floral print of yellow, black, and grass-green on a cream background.

Footstool — Buy an old one and re-cover it in same fabric as chair.

Maple rocking chair — Make chair pads in same fabric as chair.

Tab curtains — Cream with braided black trim. (You will probably have to make or have made an item as specific as this. I find you waste more time trying to find ready-made items in an exact color shade, so in the long run sewing is the most practical answer.)

Walls — Paint cream to match fabric background.

Braided rug — Yellow, green, black, and brick red.

Coffee table — Use old trunk and antique with green paint.

Lampshade — Black.

Framed print — Outdoor scene in shades of green (perhaps with a sunrise as well).

Plants — Place a couple of green plants on tables or hang from hangers.

Round table — Cover with tablecloth in accent color.

Throw pillows — Cover in accent colors from chair print.

Side tables and book case — Okay as is.

Fireplace — Paint mantle in the same antiqued green as trunk.

Here is an estimated budget for this redecorating:

Material	Estimated Cost
Fabric for chair and chair pads (11 yards at $8.00 per yard):	$88.00
Labor for slipcover for chair:	165.00
Secondhand footstool:	7.50
Fabric for curtains (1 full-size flat sheet):	9.00
Trim for curtains (10 yards at 59¢/yard):	6.00
Dowels for curtain rods and hooks:	4.50
Paint for walls and trim (4 gallons at $15 per gallon plus brush, rollers, and masking tape):	82.00
New braided rug (on sale):	75.00
Trunk (tag sale):	35.00
Lampshade:	16.00
Framed print:	35.00
Fabric for round table (5 yards at $2.25 per yard):	11.25
Throw pillows (4 at $1.00 each at a tag sale):	4.00
Total Cost:	**$538.25**

Find print or a frame at tag sale or find a frame for less than $15.00 and go to an art museum shop and purchase a print to frame. Back the print with cardboard. If necessary have a frame shop cut matting to use. The total cost should be less than $35.00.

The only way to reduce the total cost is to make your own slipcover or do the upholstery yourself, which you can learn in an adult education class. If you're a reasonably competent do-it-yourselfer, try the upholstery class.

MAKING THE MOST OF YOUR FABRIC CHOICE

When I've chosen a fabric for one element in a room, I usually think about other ways I could use it and how much I can afford to buy given the price. If the fabric isn't too costly, a few extra yards could be used for:

- A covered footstool (find one for a few dollars at the Salvation Army and cover it)
- Throw pillows for the sofa
- A tablecloth for a round table
- Adding ruffles to the edges of pillows, for a country look.

When you've selected a print fabric, you can usually introduce at least one accent color for small things in the room as well. Take color combinations from the print and repeat them in other areas of the room. When choosing paint colors, take a sample of the fabric with you. After the paint has been mixed, compare a sample paint patch with the fabric sample in natural light. If the paint color is off, have the sales clerk adjust it. If you're purchasing a premixed stock color, ask the clerk to shake the paint and give you a sample to compare with your fabric swatch.

Step 3: Develop a Plan for the Whole House, Envisioning It as a Unit

When you're developing your decorating plan, it is very important to approach your home as a total unit with individual parts. Think about repeating one or more common design elements throughout your entire living space. Contrary to some ways of thinking, I don't believe it works to decorate each room differently. A flow of color and feeling between rooms makes for a pleasant transition throughout the house, even between rooms that are physically separated from each other. The rooms shouldn't necessarily mimic each other, but they should share at least one or two design coordinators.

BLENDING ROOMS

Blending all the elements of a living space is the second most important factor (after color) in creating a unified, harmonious environment. To do this, I suggest repeating at least two of the following five design coordinators throughout most of your living space.

Wall colors. Using the same paint color on walls is the easiest way to blend rooms. Say you have a kitchen that opens into the dining room, which then flows into the living room in an L-shape. Not only is it easier to paint all the walls the same color, but it looks better. If several family living areas emanate from a central hall, consider painting the walls of the hallway and most of the rooms the same color.

You can carry out this color plan with wallpaper or paneling, as well. Once you have overall uniformity of color, different accent colors can then be used to identify defined areas. These can be introduced through fabrics, art on the walls, collectibles, and trim paint.

Flooring materials. Options include wood flooring, tile, carpeting, area rugs, and painted floors. Whatever the material used, floors should be color-coordinated, especially when they open in to each other in an area wider than the average door width. When wood floors are finished in the same wood tone (on the same living level) they create an easy flow from one room to another.

Window treatments. When one room flows and opens up into another, use the same fabric in the window treatments for both rooms. For example, in an L-shaped kitchen/dining room/living room, choose a patterned fabric for the living room that works well for floor-length drapes, then use the same fabric for some type of balloon curtains in the kitchen. The living room drapes will look formal while the kitchen curtains will look casual, but the two styles will appear coordinated.

One concern with window treatments is how they appear from the outside. The exterior windows of your house look best if they are all treated in the same way, but this doesn't always work well for interior color schemes. The solution is to use different fabrics for curtains or drapes in different rooms but toline them all with the same fabric so the exterior view is consistent (see section on making drapes beginning on page 80). You don't have to use traditional lining material; sheets (on sale) are a good and economical substitute. Or, look for appropriate material on the sale tables at fabric stores. Purchase a lightweight fabric for lining — heavier fabric could be difficult to sew when combined with the main cloth.

Similarly color-cordinated furniture and small items. One very effective way to blend the rooms in your home is to repeat a major color theme in the furniture. For instance, suppose you have an L-shaped kitchen/dining room/living room. You could blend these areas together with brick-red upholstery on the chair seats in the dining area, brick-red wing chairs and sofa and a patterned brick-red-and-blue wing chair in the living room, and a seven-foot-high kitchen cupboard (with open shelves on top) painted blue on the exterior and brick-red on the interior. This use of brick-red throughout the three areas unifies them nicely while maintaining the individuality of each.

The repetition of similar colors and/or finishes can also be accomplished through the use of certain types and colors of "smalls" (small decorative items) in various rooms. These finishes include:

- Brass (candlesticks, chandeliers, and planters)
- Iron (pots, trivets, and irons; this color can be reinforced by such items as black chairs, black lampshades, and picture frames)
- White or colored glassware (plates, lamp bases, and vases)
- Matting in picture frames
- Woodenware (boxes, shelves, and carved figurines)
- Silver (vanity sets, tea sets, bowls, and trays)
- Clear glass (shelves, bowls, and pitchers)

Adding items that are totally different and unrelated to anything else in the room adds interest, while lots of smalls that blend promote harmony.

Architectural features. The repetition of certain architectural features from one room to another will ensure continuity between adjoining rooms. These elements include:

- Detailing around doorways (door casings) and windows
- Door styles
- Ceiling moldings
- Chair railings
- Baseboards

Architectural details enhance the expression of any particular decorating style and help carry the style from room to room. Architectural detailing adds that important understated dimension to rooms. You make a style choice and then draw that architectural design element through several rooms. How much

A COMMON COLOR CHALLENGE

One of the most common color problems is two contrasting colors (for example, brick red and kelly green) used together in a room. The solution is to find a print or stripe that combines both colors and use it to cover or replace an item in need of a new look (such as a sofa, drapes, tablecloth, or bedspread).

Blending Adjoining Floor Areas

Problem: You are thinking of putting new medium-blue wall-to-wall carpeting in a hallway. The living room's wall-to-wall carpeting is chocolate-brown and in good condition. The two areas adjoin at a six-foot-wide opening. You realize that different colors at this location are not as pleasing to the eye as one continuous color flow would be. What other options exist?

Solution: To create visual flow in the space between the living room and hall, consider one of the following options:

- Buy new hallway carpeting that is exactly the same color as the living room carpet (if available).
- Choose hallway carpeting in tones of blue and brown.
- Install wood flooring in the hallway with a blue area rug.
- Paint the hallway floor in a checkerboard design using both blue and brown.

influence do architectural features have in creating a particular look? Consider two sharply contrasting styles: Victorian and Shaker. The Victorian style features elaborate moldings that are thick, wide, very intricate, and sometimes beaded (grooved). On the other hand, moldings in the Shaker style are very plain, wide, and squared off. Architectural molding is discussed in greater depth on page 43.

Step 4: Establish a Budget

Don't let a tight budget scare you away from decorating. There is always a way to achieve some level of decorating, no matter how little you can spend on it. Rarely are any of us in a position where money is no object. Tight budgets are the norm, but you can compensate by being a clever do-it-yourselfer. Think of decorating as a challenge, a game. There will be budgeting obstacles to overcome, but the reward of a lovely room will be worth the effort.

To calculate how much you can afford to spend, begin by listing everything you need to buy to accomplish the desired look. Then research how much each item costs at several different stores. If you're on a really tight budget, plan on concentrating on just one room at a time and develop a plan for purchasing items for that room over several months, if necessary.

You can itemize your budget needs on a room-by-room basis, using the chart provided (at right).

THINK OF INNOVATIVE WAYS TO SAVE

Tucking away a little money each week to build a small cash reserve will enable you to take advantage of good buys when you see them. (It's probably best not to tell *anyone* about this little cache, since other family members sometimes tend to think their own special wants are top priorities. Even $10 a week is enough to purchase paint, fabric, and some terrific garage sale items. Think of new ways you can save a few dollars, such as taking your lunch to work or saving money you'd normally spend on soda or cigarettes.

Request your birthday and holiday presents in cash or ask for items for decorating projects. On your kids' or partner's birthdays, give them presents for their rooms, such as an attractive wastepaper basket, a lamp, drapes, a desk set, a bookcase, a throw rug, a closet organizer, or pictures for the walls. This gives your children the message that you respect their rooms (notice I didn't say *clean* their rooms), and, in return, so will they. (Please, however, think carefully before allowing them to choose some wild color to paint their walls. It will likely be a passing fancy, or they will move out and you'll have to apply three coats of paint to try to cover it. If they must have something purple, let it be the bedspread or throw rug.)

When buying furnishings, look for sturdy, durable products and do quality comparison before you buy. I do not believe that "you get what you pay for" — smart shoppers can get more than they pay for, and not-so-smart shoppers can pay too much for what they get. Another way to make decorating affordable is to put items on layaway at used furniture stores, antique shops, and department stores and then make regular weekly payments.

BALANCE YOUR SPENDING

Be prudent about how you spend your money, and stick to your planned priorities. Don't impulsively spend $500 for a painting if you desperately need a carpet. Keep focused on the basic items you need to get started, and after that begin buying accessories. There is an exception to this rule: when something is either a super buy, useful, or will fill a decorating need. Say you have been saving for a dining room table and while browsing at a garage sale you spot a large Nantucket basket for $35. You know it will fill the spot on the wall in the living room and look fabulous. You also know it is a really great buy. When you know you'll probably never find such a good bargain again, weigh your options, keeping in mind that this purchase will delay getting the dining room table. Having said that, I would suggest making a pact with yourself that your next purchase will be a dining room table. To justify most purchases I make, I do have a saying, however: "It's not the things I have bought I regret; it's the things I should have bought."

Budgeting Plan

Room: _____

ITEM/JOB	COST
Furniture	
_____	_____
_____	_____
Subtotal:	_____
Recovering/slipcovers	
_____	_____
_____	_____
Subtotal:	_____
Paint	
_____	_____
_____	_____
Subtotal:	_____
Brushes & other items	
_____	_____
_____	_____
Subtotal:	_____
Window treatments	
_____	_____
_____	_____
Subtotal:	_____
Accessories	
_____	_____
_____	_____
Subtotal:	_____
Other	
_____	_____
_____	_____
Subtotal:	_____
Grand total:	_____

KEEP YOUR HOUSING COSTS REASONABLE

You don't have to have a fancy place to justify decorating. It's especially easy for young apartment dwellers to fall into the bind of paying high rent and then having very little money left for furnishings, decorating, and savings accounts. One great solution to this predicament (and a sure way to learn some decorating skills fast!) is to rent a place that is a mess on the inside and fix it up. You will save money, become more adept at such useful skills as painting and wallpapering, and gain confidence in your ability as a do-it-yourselfer.

During the first ten years of our married life, my husband and I rented several different places. After the first year in nice apartments, it occurred to us that it was going to take forever to save money to buy our first house if we didn't improve our savings plan. So we found a wreck of a house to rent. The kitchen had seven doors, three windows, and no counter space. The bathroom was old-fashioned. So many layers of wallpaper had been applied in the living and dining rooms they were literally falling off the walls. The downstairs bedroom had red, green, and blue stars on the ceiling, a floral print on the walls, and another print on the tacky linoleum. It also had no closet. The upstairs bedrooms were like the downstairs one except for the stars. Outside, the pine trees and bushes were so overgrown we couldn't see daylight.

The plus side of all this was that our rent was 75 percent less than our previous place, and the owners said we could do anything we wanted to fix it up. Before then my do-it-yourself skills were limited to sewing, but I learned to tackle all kinds of projects — building closets, painting the whole house, laying carpet, and even cutting down trees. The landlord allowed us to deduct the cost of paint from the rent, and of course my labor was free. So our only expenses were area rugs, linoleum, and some lumber. After two months, our living expenses were 75 percent lower than in our previous apartment. After six months, the house looked adorable. To this day I remember fondly the decorating experience I gained there.

Step 5: Set a Schedule for Your Decorating Work

How you schedule your decorating work depends on your personal situation, skills and interests, lifestyle, and budget.

FINDING THE TIME TO DECORATE

Just as there are food exchanges you can make with certain diets (i.e., exchange this dish for 1 starch and 1 fruit), so, too, are there "exchanges" you can make to obtain time for decorating. These are usually found after 7 or 8 P.M. when the dishes are done and the kids are in bed, or on weekends. Unfortunately, this often means trading in leisure time. After all, most of us feel that we deserve to put our feet up and watch TV after a long day's work, but exchanging this time for a decorating hour or two can yield long-term pay-offs. Long after you've forgotten that television program you didn't watch, you'll still be enjoying your beautifully decorated home. The hardest part is getting started — changing your mindset. A few years ago, at a motivational seminar, I heard a memorable quote by Brian Tracy: "There are ten two-letter words which can change your life: If it is to be, it is up to me!" These are great words for decorators (and everyone else) to live by.

Here's a general plan for scheduling time that I've found works well:

1. Formulate a decorating plan and make a list of needed supplies. For instance, say that you have analyzed your daughter's room and decided on several goals that need to be met:
   Paint the dresser.
   Mount shelf on wall for stuffed animals.
   Sew bedspread.
   Purchase small area rug.
   The materials you will need for this project include:
   1 quart of paint for dresser (use same for wall shelf)
   Paint brush (2")
   Sandpaper (fine grit)
   Brackets for mounting shelf
   Molly screws to hold in brackets
   Yardage for bedspread
   Yardage for curtains
   Thread
2. Reserve a Saturday or day off from work for collecting the necessary materials.
3. Fix an easy dinner or leftovers, and don't turn on the television if project work is scheduled.
4. After cleaning up, take a radio with you to your work area and get started.

You'll be surprised at how much you can accomplish by devoting just one hour a day to decorating work. By the end of the week you will have put in almost a whole day's work. When you need some extra motivation, invite friends to a party at your house in a month and plan to have your decorating projects completed two weeks prior to that date. Pressure is a great motivator!

PROBLEM SOLVER

Decorating on a Tight Budget

Problem: How can you get the look you want with limited resources?

Solution: Occasionally, decorating magazines feature comparison studies of two rooms that have achieved the same general look on decidedly different budgets. If the magazines can do it, so can you. You can capture the same overall color scheme and feeling of an expensively appointed room by installing more modest furnishings that don't look "cheap." Some examples of less expensive substitutions that won't compromise the overall look of a room include:

Sofa — Purchase one filled with Dacron instead of down.

Drapes — Make your own pleater-tape drapes (see page 82) with $3-per-yard fabric rather than readymade ones.

Paintings — Search for attractive prints and quaint old frames at junk shops rather than purchasing oil paintings by well-known artists.

Porcelain — Use copies instead of the real thing.

THE IMPORTANCE OF PLANNING AHEAD

When you're trying to get a lot done in a limited amount of time, there's no substitute for making a detailed materials list and schedule of tasks. To make the most of the time you have for a project, purchase all the necessary materials before beginning so you'll be sure to have everything you will need on hand. If you live in a small town, call suppliers and ask if the desired material is in stock and, if not, how long is the lead time? (Suppliers from paint and plumbing shops tend to be conservative about carrying inventory.) Calling ahead can prevent spending a Saturday morning getting to the paint shop only to be told your specific color isn't available.

You'll be surprised at how effective you can make your decorating time if you are able to get right into the actual task at hand. A few years ago my mother-in-law was upset with the way the interior of her 1790s house looked. She liked my decorating style, so I proposed a plan: If she allowed me to do anything I wanted and paid for the materials, I would go and stay at her house and do the work. She agreed. My mother-in-law lived two hours away so I had to assemble very accurate materials lists ahead of time.

I made a preliminary trip to her house to organize a room-by-room plan for all projects and write down measurements. The jobs included painting, window treatments, and miscellaneous decorating accents. One of my challenges was to make sense of a mantel that had simply been stuck on a blank wall with no fireplace opening. I decided to leave the mantel there and make it look realistic by applying brick facing around the perimeter of the interior opening and hearth and painting the "chimney box" black. My materials list for this project included all the building materials as well as accessories such as fireplace tools and a screen.

To finish off the effect, I painted the white mantel brick red and repeated this brick red color theme for the window frame trim and a print for the curtains in the room. I made the curtains ahead of time at my house. The effect was dramatic and she loved it.

Decorating Schedule

Room: _____

PROJECTS TO ACCOMPLISH	TIME FRAME							
	Month ____				Month ____			
	Week				Week			
	1	2	3	4	1	2	3	4
Carpentry								
Wall Paint								
Trim Paint								
Flooring								
Window Treatments								
Buy Furniture								
Upholster Furniture								
Buy Accessories								
Redo Accessories								

The fireplace was just one of a number of projects accomplished in about 4½ days of continual, focused work. My plan, schedule, and materials list made all the difference. As part of your decorating planning, think through each small step and write down all materials (even the ones you think you have). Then go to your workshop and check partially used products to be sure that the product is still okay — like wood putty that might have hardened.

Before the first work day, write down a step-by-step plan for each part of the project. Be specific. As you write down this detailed plan and the schedule, simultaneously make a list of the materials you'll need to complete each step. Here's a sample step-by-step plan.

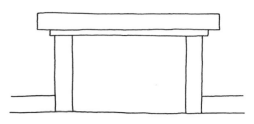

With careful advance planning, I was able to do the work of transforming a fake mantel on a blank wall (above) into a real-looking fireplace in just 1 day (below).

Job: Painting Room

Date or day	Steps to take
Wednesday after work	1. Make list of materials needed and purchase (buy materials by certain date).
Thursday evening	2. Remove all small items in room and window treatments.
Friday evening	3. Remove all furniture in room.
Saturday A.M.	4. Protect floor. Patch holes in wall and sand.
Saturday A.M.	5. Tape off woodwork.
Saturday P.M.	6. Paint walls.
Sunday	7. Paint woodwork.
Monday	8. Scrape and wash windows.
Monday	9. Replace furniture in room.
Tuesday	10. Replace window treatments and small items.

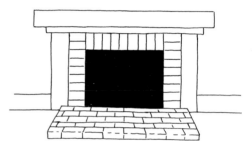

Project Completion Date: To help determine an attainable deadline for completing the whole project, write down realistic daily work completion projections on a calendar (such as the steps outlined above). Breaking down a project into parts and then being able to cross off each step as it's completed is a major psychological boost. If you can feel the satisfaction of completing part of the job, the rest won't feel so overwhelming.

Angling pieces of furniture, such as this desk, can help break up a large space into several more intimate living spaces.

Making the Most of What You've Got (or Can Get Inexpensively)

Now that you've identified your preferred style and color scheme (as discussed in Chapter 1), what do you do with the objects, furniture, and fabrics you already own that don't fit this new look? Don't chuck them just yet. Try to take a fresh approach to each piece and think creatively about how it might be transformed. For instance, a piece may take on a whole new look when it is:

- Given a new location
- Painted or stained
- Added to another piece you have or find, or subtracted from a piece it is already attached to.

Sometimes you need to take drastic measures to get yourself to look at what you have in a new way.

Rearrange and Reuse What You've Got

One good way to get a fresh perspective on a room in your house is to literally move everything you can lift out of the room — lamps, vases, decorative glassware, and all items hanging on the walls. Now walk through your house and pick up anything from other rooms that might remotely fit into a new arrangement in the room in question. Add these things to the collection you removed from the room.

REARRANGE THE LARGE ITEMS

With all the small pieces and accessories gone, take a critical look at the arrangement of the basic furniture left in the room, such as sofas, large chairs, and tables, and think of other ways they might be arranged. A good way to experiment with various alternatives is to draw the room to scale on graph paper, allowing 1 square to equal 1 foot of room space. (For a larger scale, allow two squares to equal 1 foot, taping together several sheets of paper if necessary.) Mark where all the windows and doors are located. Then cut out blocks, again to scale, to represent each piece of large furniture, and try various arrangements on your plan

How do you decide what is the best place to position a large piece of furniture? Some pieces, such as a sofa, fit in only one place — thus the best place is the only place. A large piece of furniture should balance any built-in features. For example: You have a fireplace with a mantel on the east side of the living room. The east wall is 24′ long, leaving enough wall space for a large hutch, but would you put one there? Most likely not. The fireplace and mantel, which serve as a large focal point, should be balanced by placing the hutch on the opposite wall or as close to the opposite wall as possible.

Position large pieces first and then work around them. A successful furniture arrangement should feature the following:

■ Convenience — each piece in a place where it is most functional

■ Balance — a setup that is pleasing to the eye and promotes an overall balanced look to the room

■ A focal point — a distinctive area of concentrated vision, such as a large piece of furniture or a small piece used in combination with other small items to create a mass (see page 23).

Consider all the possible arrangements for your room. For instance, try angling some of the furniture; it does not always have to be pushed flat against the wall or at right angles to it. Just as kitchens frequently have peninsulas, so, too, can your living room.

Think about how you use the space and arrange the furniture to meet those purposes. To create an intimate conversation area, try positioning two or three upholstered chairs very close together. Balance this by pushing the sofa a distance away, depending on the size of the room. Or, group two sectional sofas and a wingback sofa (all slipcovered in the same fabric) in a U-shape.

Don't be afraid to think outside present room boundaries. You can move furniture from one room to another. Just because that pink chest has always been in your daughter's bedroom doesn't mean it has to stay there forever. If you're looking for an accent piece for the family room and realize that the chest is a little too small for all your daughter's clothes, don't be afraid to move it and give it a new look. If painting the chest brick red would make it perfect for the family room, do it and find a new piece for your daughter's room.

One of the most unusual uses to which I've put furniture in an arrangement occured when I remodeled a house that did not have a formal dining room. What was I going to do with my gorgeous Queen Anne–style 42″-round table? Being one of my favorite pieces, it was certainly not going out on "permanent" loan to my dear daughter. (She thinks I've forgotten about the secretary desk I loaned her.) But then I came up with the idea of putting the table in our very large (17′x19′) master bedroom. Although I was sure it was going to be just another pretty piece, we ended up using that table much more than we'd expected.

CREATE FOCAL POINTS

As you consider various arrangements of your large pieces, think about creating a central unit within the room — a focal point that draws the eye immediately to it. Every room should have a focal point, either a color accent or an arrangement "hog" that takes up most of the space, extending from floor to almost-ceiling height.

A focal point can be a contrasting piece of furniture (such as a piece painted in a color complementary to yet dramatically different from the other furniture) or an extra large piece of furniture (entertainment center, secretary desk, corner cupboard). A cabinet displaying an eye-catching collection can also be a focal point, as can a wall hanging or picture positioned over a piece of furniture. Groupings of anything — tall potted plants, hanging plants, or birdhouses, both standing and hanging — are effective focal points. How do you know if you have an effective focal point? Visitors will walk in and say, "Wow!"

ADD LARGE WALL ACCESSORIES

Once you've positioned the large pieces of furniture in your room arrangement, you are ready for the smaller pieces. These include side tables for lamps, chairs, and the like and should be positioned at the same time as wall accessories such as paintings and pictures, quilts, mirrors, and whatever else you own and want to display. Try placing the wall accessories in close enough proximity to pieces of furniture so they act as a unit. Used jointly and in harmony with the smaller pieces of furniture, large wall accessories can balance larger furniture or any architectural focal point.

Color works particularly well as a unifying theme. Don't worry if the elements don't match exactly as long as the overall color effect is consistent. If

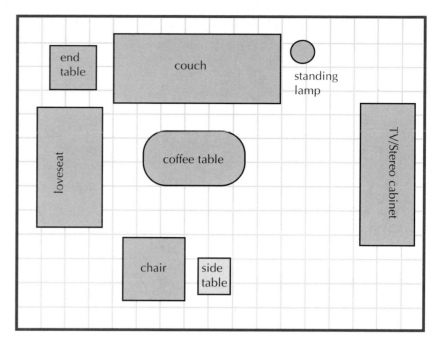

Creating a scaled drawing of your room and scaled pieces to represent the basic pieces of furniture allows you to experiment with different arrangements without actually moving a thing.

This chandelier hung in a corner creates an unexpected focal point.

Grouping a number of small framed pieces together creates a striking overall effect that is equivalent to one large painting.

you have a picture (or a frame) you like but the color isn't quite compatible, consider how you might change this by painting the frame, adding a color mat, or finding a print or painting with more suitable tones.

The two key elements to be aware of when selecting large wall accessories to complement selected pieces of furniture are dimension and color. The dimensions of the piece should be compatible with the piece of furniture it hangs over. If it's not large enough, try hanging other, smaller objects near it to create a more massive effect.

If you don't have a large wall accessory, the same unit effect can be achieved by grouping together several smaller pieces that are similar in color or type. For example, you could frame a variety of personal mementos in inexpensive small black frames. These might include special greeting cards you've received, reproductions of wonderful paintings cut out of high-quality magazines (such as *Antiques* and *Architectural Digest)*, photographs, postcards, or special notes from your children. I have a collection hanging above my desk that includes a beautiful Fraktur (greeting card in calligraphy) that my honey made for my birthday, a signed thank-you note from Barbara Bush, a wonderful printed sen-

timent about friends given to me by my dear friend Diana, a folk-art wood burning on a slice of log made by my sister, Frances, and other cherished mementos.

Taken singly, these personal items would never make a decorating statement, but, mounted in black frames and integrated as a unit, they look terrific. Moreover, these treasures are there for me to see, not stuck in a dark drawer where they're too often forgotten.

Placement is very important. Group the frames closely together (with 1″ or less between them). You might feel more comfortable laying out your arrangement on a table first to get it just right before you hang it on the wall. If you have a number of square and rectangular shapes in a wall grouping, try adding something round for a refreshing change.

ADD THE WINDOW TREATMENTS

Once you're satisfied with the arrangement of your furniture and large accent pieces, it's time to focus on window treatments, if you plan to use them. You might ask, why do the window treatments before arranging the small items in the room? The answer is that the volume of color and texture added by curtains or draperies makes an amazing difference in the feel of the entire room and will affect your decisions about where to locate the smalls. If, however, you know it's going to take some time to get the window treatments up, go ahead and arrange your smalls, keeping in mind that you may need to adjust them later when the curtains or drapes are in place. (For guidelines on selecting and making window treatments, see pages 35 to 38.)

ARRANGE THE SMALL ITEMS

Now's the time to start bringing back into the room all those small items you took out. Begin by arranging the practical items whose locations are dictated by their functions, such as:

- Lamp next to a reading chair
- Footstool next to a recliner
- Freestanding lamp near the sofa
- Afghan on the rocker
- Throw pillows on the sofa

Once you've placed all such items in their appropriate spots, fill in the open spaces that are calling out for something more. Bring in other smalls you have such as plants, silk flower arrangements, candlesticks, books, a fruit bowl, or pretty dishes.

Collecting a variety of similar items, such as pewterware, is fun to do and creates a handsome display. Try hanging pieces on the interior side walls of a cabinet to create a sense of depth.

Hanging Objects on the Wall

Problem: You're ready to make a wall display of your treasured pictures but you are worried about making holes in the wall.

Solution: I hear more stories of people who avoid hanging things because they don't want to make holes in the wall. This seems to especially bother the man in the house. I say, what are you saving the walls for, anyhow?

For lightweight items, use small picture-hanging nails and hooks. If you place a nail in a position that's not quite right, pull it out and make another hole. The extra hole will most likely be covered up by the picture or can be filled with a little taping compound.

The easiest method for hanging any object weighing more than two pounds is to use large picture-hanging hooks. These come in a variety of sizes according to the weight they will hold. The nail (packaged with the hook) slides through the hole in the hook and enters the wall at an angle. The hole left is small and easy to fill.

If hooks and nails aren't strong enough for a heavy mirror, use a molly screw. (See page 110 for directions.)

As you arrange your smalls, try to achieve an overall balanced look. Say you have a corner cupboard in which you would like to display a glass collection. However, when you leave the cupboard door open, it hangs in front of a stair railing and appears out of kilter or off-balance. You can create a sense of balance by hanging a planter piece from the glass collection on the wall beside the cupboard. This piece repeats the pattern shown in the cupboard and draws the eye to the side, balancing the cupboard door.

THE JOYS OF COLLECTING SMALL ITEMS

Collections of smalls personalize and add dimension to your decorating. There are many possibilities for collecting: baskets, stuffed animals, dishes, plants in wall containers, old woodenware, tinware, and pieces of embroidery and crewelwork. Even though you may not have a lot of room or a lot of money, or think you may have no interest in collecting, trust me — you'll get hooked.

To begin a collection, find a fairly insignificant object that you like and buy two of them. Find one more and you are a collector. You might not even realize that you've started a collection, but when you do, you'll find that you'll get excited by every find of a new addition to the collection. This will give you a focus when you go shopping and others will know what to buy you as a gift. Once you've assembled a critical mass of objects, you'll have a fabulous decorating accent. It's also great fun to create a collection for someone else. If you are at a loss when buying birthday or holiday presents for others, find an affordable item of interest to them and start collecting. Here are some examples of how collections can be used and/or displayed:

- Teapots on a high shelf around kitchen
- Books on any type of shelves
- Iron trivets attractively arranged on a wall
- Any kind of glassware on cupboard shelves
- Old tools hanging on a wall in a rustic room
- Porcelain animals grouped on top of a chest
- Plants clustered together on a wicker plant stand
- Needlepoint pillows arranged on a sofa
- Three-inch candle holders with candles in various heights and colors
- Numerous pieces of child-size furniture positioned in a very small area
- Brass bells grouped on the floor next to a door
- Glass bottles on glass shelves in front of a window
- Perfume bottles on mirrored tray on dresser
- Marbles in glass jars in children's room
- Baseball cards under glass on desktop and in matching albums on shelves
- Hats, caps, or T-shirts with messages on them hung on walls

If you need just a bit more pattern or color in a room, one easy way to introduce it is with boxes covered with wallpaper or fabric. These are quite easy to make from scratch (information is available in craft catalogs), or you can buy unfinished ones in a variety of sizes and shapes. You can also easily create a lampshade to match your decor. Lampshade kits are available with an adhesive surface; all you have to do is apply a cover in the fabric of your choice — a twenty-minute job.

Think creatively about ways to group or display small items for maximum effect. For example, try grouping several clear-glass candlestick holders (with color-coordinated candles) on a mirrored tabletop or shelf. If you have some very small items in a display cupboard, hang part of the collection on the interior cupboard walls. This makes the collection look fuller. You can create a sense of greater depth in open cupboards with dishes or a pewter collection by hanging cups, measures, or spoons on the inside cupboard walls.

Using Plants in Decorating

If you love plants, then I encourage you to decorate with them to your heart's content. They make great fillers for spots needing a bit of color or balance. The only potential problem is when you overwater them and the water marks a piece of furniture or the floor. But you can avoid this by using deep saucers and a small plastic mat under the saucers. Some effective ways to use plants include:

- Massing them together to create a dramatic and beautiful focal point. Combine a birdbath, birdhouse, and hanging plants for a charming vignette. Install a recirculating pump in a fountain for real drama.
- Creating a natural screen in large open windows.
- As a "furnishing" in a large built-in planter. A six-foot-long planter in front of a picture window is gorgeous.

A grouping of plants makes an appealing focal point in an entranceway.

- Arranging plants in clay or decorated pots up a staircase to add color and interest.
- Grouping hanging plants in the bathroom for a lively accent.
- Creating a minigarden on the floor in front of a south-facing window.

Thoroughly waterproof the floor with a couple of layers of 6-millimeter plastic brought up over the edges of 2"x 4" framing. Cover the plastic with decorative small stones and set potted plants in saucers among the stones. (In case of spills the floor is protected, and it's a nice look.) Create a garden that fits your look, color, and tastes. Choices include: herbs, orchids, cactus, or a variety of philodendron and ivy and so forth. I have had six azalea plants in a large planter for over a year, and they still look healthy and have bloomed three times. Small fruit trees are super for those who can grow them. An indoor garden is especially enjoyable for people who spend a lot of time at home.

Finding and Using Secondhand Furnishings

Once you've found a new arrangement for your "old" belongings, you'll probably have some ideas for additional pieces you would like to purchase, either to complement the new look or fill in empty spaces. A great way to obtain new pieces *and* keep to a tight budget is to search for secondhand treasures at such places as discount stores, garage sales, Salvation Army and Goodwill stores, auctions, your mom's attic, bazaars, antique shops, used furniture stores, and through classified newspaper ads.

Be patient. You never know where you'll find the perfect thing — it will surprise you! Make the search part of your routine. Stop in regularly at the Salvation Army, used furniture stores, antique shops, or consignment shops (otherwise known as the goody stores) you pass on your daily route. When you visit often, you can be in and out in 5 minutes because you know the merchandise and can quickly spot what's new.

In some of these places you can barter for a better price. If you're not good at this, team up with someone who is until you get comfortable. It takes courage and practice. Remember, all someone can say is "No, you can't have the vase for $5. The asking price is $10." But they might say "I'll split the difference and sell it to you for $7.50."

Another way to acquire a new piece is to trade in one of your own — put a piece of furniture or article you are not crazy about on consignment and use the money to get something you like better. I once had an ornate sterling silver napkin ring. I wasn't interested in starting a napkin ring collection, so I traded it in at an antique shop, and I've never regretted it.

BUYING THE BASICS SECONDHAND

If you're just starting out and don't have any furniture yet, you can find many of your basic decorating needs at secondhand shops. To begin with, if you're looking for a sofa, search newspaper classified ads, used furniture stores, and the Salvation Army shop. You will pay the lowest price if the fabric on an upholstered sofa is torn or dirty. As long as the piece feels sturdy and the cushions do not have worn depressions, you can transform it with a simple slipcover. (A few years ago I got the cutest little wingback sofa at the Salvation Army for $35. It was in such good condition it could have been used "as is." I had a particular color scheme in mind, so I had a slipcover made for $125, and it's still great.) You can buy ready-made slipcovers, have them made, or make your own.

Seamstresses who make slipcovers will usually come to your house and take measurements. With fabric in hand, they go back to their shop, cut and sew, and then bring the slipcovers for a fitting. After making the final adjustments, the seamstress brings back the finished slipcovers and puts them on the furniture. Fabric can be purchased by you or through them at an additional charge.

Of course, it will save you a lot of time and work if you can find a used sofa in fair enough condition that you don't have to re-cover it. Or, for a studio apartment, buy a used twin bed and cover it with a tailored bedspread in fabric suitable for a living room. Just toss a lot of throw pillows across the back.

WHERE TO FIND WHAT INEXPENSIVELY

If you're just starting out in your first apartment or house, you may be overwhelmed by your furniture needs. Don't panic: You can find many things secondhand or at discount that will serve you well until you can invest in something more permanent.

Lamps are usually readily available in secondhand shops or discount stores or at garage sales. Lampshades alone cost so much that it is often worthwhile to buy the whole lamp. Discount stores have fairly good basic glass lamps for nominal sums.

For a small lamp table, check first in used furniture stores. If you can't find anything in your price range, buy a

---

PROBLEM SOLVER

Creating a Dining Room "Set" With What You've Got

Problem: What do you do if you've moved into a house with a dining room but don't have proper dining room furniture or the money to buy it?

Solution: Try using outdoor furniture indoors and make it look as if it belongs. Black cast-iron patio furniture can be used in a dining room; even an inexpensive picnic table can look nice when covered with a floor-length tablecloth of fabric that matches or complements the desired look. You can even make matching pads for the benches or chairs, or buy unmatched wooden chairs at garage sales and paint or stain them to give them a new look. Painting each chair a different color or pattern can add an offbeat note to the room. A heavy-duty card table can be dressed up with a skirt and a glass top, and covers can be made for the four chairs with a coordinated fabric. The secret is to make it look as if the arrangement is deliberate rather than makeshift or temporary.

A cast-iron patio table can be dressed up to become a temporary dining room table.

cardboard decorator table or a barrel cut in half and cover it with a fabric skirt. Buy a length of fabric cut to length and drape it (without sewing).

For a coffee table, you can use any wooden box of the right size. Two barrel halves set side by side are another option, perhaps with a piece of heavy board or heavy glass laid across the top.

To furnish the bedroom, I suggest checking with new furniture stores and asking if they have any damaged box spring and mattress sets. For a modest sum you can get a metal frame, as well. A headboard isn't necessary. You can usually find a good chest of drawers at a used furniture store.

For a nightstand, use any small table. A candlestand will work, even though it doesn't have drawers. You can also fashion one out of a secondhand decorator table by covering it with a sheet that matches your bed comforter. Or, you can even try spray painting or sponge painting a file cabinet to match your bedroom colors. You'll have space for a plant on the top and personal things in the drawers.

Need a table and chairs? Buy them at a used furniture store. Or buy a card table or outdoor furniture. Both can be covered with a pretty tablecloth. If you buy an old kitchen table with an awful-colored Formica top, spray-paint the legs and apply Con-Tact paper on the tabletop. It lasts a long time. Or, find a table with a base that is in good condition, even if the top is damaged. Then just paint the top to match your kitchen colors.

For a home office, you can create a desk from two file cabinets set 25″ to 30″ apart. Cut a piece of ⅝″ plywood (smooth on one side) to match the depth and the length (approximately 5′) of the file cabinets. You can make a fabric skirt by gathering fabric uniformly and attaching it with a hot-glue gun to the edge of the wood. To determine the yardage needed, measure around the four sides of the desk top and then double that length. For example, a 40″-long desk that is 20″ on each side has a total perimeter measurement of 120″. For a skirt, this desk would require 240″, or 6¾ yards (240″ divided by 36″). Finish the plywood desktop by covering it with Con-Tact paper.

Creating Storage Space for Every Room

Storage space is achieved in two ways: By placing things in drawers, and by placing things on shelves (open or behind doors). These are the only options. The trick is to do this attractively.

One of the most practical and versatile pieces of furniture you can find at most secondhand shops is a chest of drawers (also known as a "case piece"). Substantial case pieces with drawers or shelves are useful in every room of the house.

Storage space is obviously important for the bedroom, but it's just as important in all the other rooms. If your kitchen has insufficient storage space, install a chest of drawers or a step-back cupboard (the bottom portion is deeper than the top portion). Use a chest of drawers in the dining room for storage in addition to or in place of a china cabinet. Cupboards and desks work well in the living room to hold everything from books and photo albums to games and hobby materials. In the entrance hall, a tall chimney cupboard is handy for to holding gloves, scarves, hats, and so on.

You can adapt a secondhand case piece to fit the room you put it in. A typical bedroom dresser won't look like the missing piece of a bedroom set once you've given it a fresh coat of paint. Paint a four-drawer bureau in an accent color and put it in the kitchen to hold silverware and linens. A paint job can make an old beat-up fall-front desk with shelves so dazzling it can serve as a focal point in the living room. A new trend in kitchen design is to install a piece of cabinetry that is different from the rest of the cupboards and looks like a piece of furniture. It could even *be* a piece of furniture.

In addition to giving you more storage space, a case piece automatically becomes a focal point when painted in an accent color. Just be careful to select a color that fits well into your color scheme. If you're not sure about a color, paint or spray it on a large piece of cardboard first and place it where the piece of furniture will ultimately go. Live with the cardboard in place for a few days and you'll soon know if it's the right color. If you decide the tone is right but it's just a little too bright, use the dabbing trick again. Squirt some burnt sienna or burnt umber artist's oil color on a rag and rub it on the piece. Then wipe it off with a a clean rag a little at a time until you're pleased with the color. Finish with a coat of clear polyurethane or varnish.

REMODELING A PIECE OF OLD FURNITURE

Another way to transform an old piece of furniture and make it more useful is to add onto it. For instance, you can make a desk from a low chest of drawers (approximately 38″ tall).

A desk. Use a piece of ⅝″ plywood (smooth on one side) to cover the top. Cut the plywood the same length as the chest (so it will fit flush with the sides) and at least 4″ wider than the measurement of the chest from front to back. Position the plywood over the top of the chest, allowing a 4″ overhang in the front to make a comfortable writing surface.

Nail or screw the plywood in place on top of the chest. Add a ⅝″ edging of wood or molding around the edge of the plywood. Fill in the screw holes with putty and paint the new writing surface to match the chest.

Position a set of shelves on the back 8″ of your new desk. If you have wider shelving, you may want to allow for the plywood to overhang the back of the chest. You can create a similar effect by fastening shelves on the wall above the desk, leaving a 6″ to 8″ space on the wall between the desktop and the shelves.

You can create a "secretary-like" desk from an old chest of drawers by adding a plywood top that extends over the front.

An alternative version of a modified secretary desk.

You can also make a modified version of a secretary desk from a fall-front desk. Just find a set of shelves that are the same width or narrower than the top of the desk itself (most fall-front desks are usually 10″ deep). Attach the shelves to the desk to complete the project.

A vanity base. A mahogany buffet can be converted to a vanity base for a powder room sink. Fasten the drawer in front of the sink area permanently close and run plumbing pipes through the base; cut a hole in the top to hold the sink and finish the top with marble tile.

An entertainment center. Add doors to a cupboard with open shelves to make a cabinet for the television, stereo equipment, and other audio-visual equipment.

A bedroom set. It's amazing how creative you can be when you're desperate. I once needed a very tall chest of drawers for my daughter's room. (There was no closet in the room.) Buying a fancy chest-on-chest was out of the question financially. So I found two identical four-drawer chests — at two separate antique shops in two different states — that both had spool decorations. (Spool design was among the earliest woodworking styles to be mechanically cut in America.) I paid $10 for one chest and $30 for the other. When I got them home, I proceeded to rip the top off one chest and saw the bottom off the other. Then I married the two, one on top of the other. Voilà! I had my chest-on-chest, with spool decoration running up the front to tie the whole thing together. (See photo at right.)

To match the spool chest, I then modified a Jenny Lind spool bed, a style popular during the 1800s. Thousands of these beds were made and are still readily available in used furniture and antique shops. They are usually inexpensive. I paid $2 for mine and then worked weeks removing the old shellac. I then converted the low poster bed to a canopy bed. (See photo.) How? First I cut the 4 finials off the posts, took them to a cabinet shop, and had 4 3′ spool posts turned that matched the diameter of the finials. I had holes drilled into both ends of each spool post and steel dowels inserted so that the posts would set on top of each spool post. The addition of the newly turned 3′ post on top of the original spool post raises the height so that a canopy fits in the right proportion. The wooden canopy frame fits over the steel dowel. The finial slides down on the remainder of the steel dowel. I couldn't find a wooden canopy frame in a ¾ size (the width of this bed) so I purchased a double one. It is relatively easy to reduce the width of a canopy by cutting off the slats and cutting down the ends and redrilling holes in the ends.

You can convert any bed with posts on four corners into a canopy bed. The new posts don't have to be spool-turned; simple rounded posts are just as effective. Antique beds are usually pretty good buys. They are frequently too narrow to accommodate a double mattress, so you may have to do a little retrofitting to get a mattress to fit. Some mattress companies will make a ¾-sized mattress (to your specifications) for the same price as a

The tall chest of drawers was created by stacking and joining two short, matching dressers. The Jenny Lind spool bed was transformed into a canopy bed by the addition of matching spooled posts which the original finials fit on top of.

double mattress of equal quality. If the bed was constructed to hold the mattress down between the two outer rails, you can adapt it by one of the following methods:

- Set blocks of wood on the side rails to bring the mattress above the bedframe.
- Replace the original bed slats with very thick ones that will lift the mattress above the side rails.
- Place a sheet of ⅝″ plywood on top of the side rails and put the mattress on top of the plywood. This arrangement makes for a firm but comfortable sleeping surface.

Getting the Basics Right

Windows, Walls, Moldings, Doors, and Floors

Creating the look you want involves more than furniture and furnishings. The way you treat your windows, walls, moldings, doors, and floors is central to the overall appearance of your rooms.

Finding Window Treatments to Fit Your Look

The possibilities for creative design with window treatments are unlimited. The color, pattern, texture, and sheer volume of curtains, drapes, or shades can dramatically alter the look of a home, and often for a relatively modest sum of money. Hitting on the right window treatments is key to achieving the particular look you desire.

Several factors should be considered before you decide on window treatments. Ask yourself the questions on the following page.

- Is the look I want elegant or casual?
- Do I need window treatments for privacy?
- Would a particular color or pattern pull the overall look together?
- Does the window treatment need to be custom made or can it be purchased as a ready made?

DECIDING ON A STYLE

Your choice of fabric will depend in part on the style of curtain you select — floor-length drapes, valances, or tab curtains. The style should complement the overall look. Are you aiming for elegance, or a homier, more casual feel? You may think "elegant" implies greater expense than "casual," but it's amazing how you can attain a certain look in an unexpected way. Elegant-looking drapes can be made out of expensive velvet, but they don't have to be. I have a friend who made some beautiful drapes out of muslin. To cover her 12′-wide window, she sewed together several floor-length panels of unlined muslin, then added a 10″ border strip of blue calico near the bottom that coordinated with the rest of her color scheme. The result was striking.

On the other hand, tab-style curtains are casual, but if made out of a stitched crewel fabric they would be quite costly. So, you see, elegant does not necessarily mean more expensive, nor does casual mean less expensive.

SELECTING FABRIC

Selecting a fabric that pulls together the various elements of the room is the most important aspect of window treatment. When you've got the right fabric, the result is dynamite.

Knowing what type of fabric might work well in a particular room is a skill that's honed by experience. There is no right or wrong as far as fabrics go, if the cloth does what you want it to. I don't believe in being confined by the narrow "definition" of a given fabric. Never one to follow the book, I've experimented with unlikely fabrics such as corduroy — and even burlap — for drapes; I've used dress fabrics for curtains and drapery fabrics for dresses. Sheets can be used for drapes or curtains. Upholstery fabric, however, is generally too heavy for either drapes or curtains.

Learning about fabrics can be done through trial and error. Ask the opinion of a knowledgeable seamstress about the idiosyncrasies of particular fabric types. Or, go ahead and experiment, and then ask yourself:
- Does the fabric look right when finished?
- Was the fabric impossible to work with?

Satin or real velvet frays easily, making you want to scream as you try to work with it. Some fabrics are so stiff or bulky that you can't get them to hang nicely.

The style of window treatments should complement the overall look of the room.

I once made a swag and jabot curtain out of a heavy creweled fabric. I had a devil of a time trying to get the folds to hang correctly because of the thickness of the crewelwork. You'll run into fewer problems with midweight fabric.

CREATING PRIVACY

What purpose will your window treatments serve? This factor affects your choice of fabric. A very sheer fabric, for instance, would not be appropriate if privacy is an issue.

Window treatments designed for privacy must be easy to open and close. This generally requires some type of traverse rod. Traverse rods should be installed before you purchase or hem any drapes, since you cannot know the proper length for hemming until you actually hang the drapes on the rod or measure for the finished length once the rod is up.

Another style that is easy to operate is a decorative pole and drapes hung with large rings. Pleats are folded in the fabric at specified increments, and the rings are sewn to the back of the pleats. A clear plastic handle, or baton, is attached to the end ring in the middle of the window to facilitate opening and closing the drape. To open the drapes, you simply push the baton toward the center of the window; to close them, pull it to the side. This style works well if you have a limited number of windows and can easily stand in front of them to reach the baton. However, if a large piece of furniture is in front of the window, you may find this device too awkward.

If you are thinking of using sheer curtains across an entire

Pleated drapes hung on large rings are a good choice for windows where you want to be able to open and close the curtains easily.

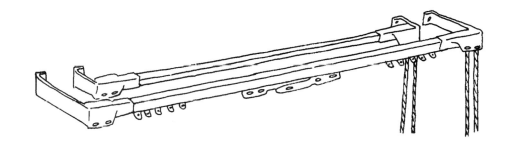

Two traverse rods of varied widths can be mounted at the same height to accommodate both sheer curtains and drapes hung across a wide window or group of windows.

window but occasionally would like to open them for direct sunlight, you need a traverse rod. A separate rod would be required for a second set of drapes on either side of the sheer curtains. Traverse rods come in adjustable depths so you can easily mount two at the same height. Curtain rods also come in adjustable widths and depths, which allows for mounting both curtains and a ruffled valance. (See page 98 for an overview of curtain rods.)

MAKING YOUR OWN WINDOW TREATMENTS

When it comes to window treatments, I strongly recommend using (or developing) your basic sewing skills. Having your choices limited to ready-made draperies and curtains is extremely frustrating. Much of my furniture is simple reproductions, so what makes my decorating unique and adds personality to my rooms is largely my handmade window treatments.

You can have draperies custom-made at a decorating shop or find a local seamstress to do the job. But don't be so quick to look for someone else to do it. *You* can sew! Making curtains isn't like making clothing or doing tailoring. All it requires is that you master the basic technique of sewing straight-stitch seams. Sew pleater tape onto your selected fabric with a straight seam and you've made your own custom drapes! (See pages 80 to 82 for full instructions on making pleater-tape drapes.)

If you've ever gone drapery-fabric shopping, you know that the main focus is not to save money but to find "it" — the perfect fabric for a particular room. Ordinary drapes come in basic colors and sizes. If manufacturers produced a broad enough range of draperies to fit the specialized color tastes and window sizes of everyone, their inventory would be staggering. As a result, searching for a finished window treatment in a particular color print is often futile.

Your chances of finding just what you're looking for are enhanced tremendously by going to a fabric store. To fabric hunters, large fabric stores are a little bit of heaven. Keeping focused on the purpose that brought you there is the biggest challenge; the distractions are many. There's that stupendous wool stripe, that lovely toile, or that delightful polished cotton print that would look just right in your bathroom.

There's no doubt about it: I'm a fabric junkie. Oh, yes, there are plenty like me. We hide fabric in our closets and under the beds. I "need" three more houses to decorate just to use up my fabric inventory. But that doesn't mean I resist another fabric store sale. There's always room for a little bit more. If my confession inspires any of you who have always purchased ready-made curtains to consider buying fabric, then my habit has served a larger purpose. Is buying fabric more trouble? Well, yes. Is making your own drapes or curtains less expensive? Absolutely, especially when you find wonderful bargains! Complete instructions for making a range of simple curtains, from no-sew swags to pleated drapes, are included in Chapter 6.

Wall Treatments

Paint or wallpaper are the obvious ways to cover walls, but there are other options that can add to your decorating statement, creating a distinctive look. These include textured paint, fabric, stenciling, mural painting, heavily embossed wallpaper, papering ceilings (lot of angles), brick facing, and paneling with pine boards. There are two reasons you may want to use one of these "special-effect" techniques: To cover up walls in poor condition and to create drama. Disguising damaged walls is one way to put off repairing or replacing wallboard or plaster.

TEXTURED PAINT

Applying textured paint is one of the least expensive options for covering uneven wall surfaces. I've covered over several layers of wallpaper by applying this thick, grainy paint with a brush. Before beginning to paint, be sure that any existing wallpaper is fastened securely to the wall so it doesn't pull away. If you do find any loose paper, either tear sections off or refasten it with wallpaper glue.

Where you tear off paper, simply apply a heavier coat of textured paint there to even out the imperfect wall surface. This technique is particularly good when you want to avoid extensive wallpaper stripping. Tearing old wallpaper off in just the loose spots goes quickly — it's removing every last particle of wallpaper and preparing the wall surface for a flat wall paint that is time-consuming, and often impossible if the wall has been patched as well.

If you are applying textured paint to a previously painted surface, you need to know what type of paint you are covering. Many oil paints are completely incompatible with latex-based textured paint. Before you can apply latex paint over oil paint, you must apply a primer. I learned this lesson the hard way.

In one of my houses, the dining room walls and ceilings were in terrible condition. I decided I would hide the imperfections. The textured paint had worked so well for me on wallpaper surely it would again! I read the label and noted that a primer should be used if the surface to be painted was oil. I had no way of knowing what was on the walls and ceiling and was impatient to move along with the project. So the first day I painted the ceiling. The paint went on easily and looked great.

The next morning I peeked in to look at my good work and was shocked! It looked like a scene right out of a horror movie — the paint was dripping off the ceiling in long strings. It was the worst mess imaginable. Those extra minutes it would have taken to prime would have saved me two days of scraping, and several hours of clean-up.

WALLPAPERING TIPS

If you have an old house where the floors slope and walls are slightly crooked, don't use a striped wallpaper on the walls since it tends to accentuate the crookedness.

If you have a room with angled ceilings, use a printed wallpaper that has a light background. Apply the wallpaper to the ceiling side of the angle and make curtains that match the wallpaper. The result will be that the angles will appear to recede.

USING FABRIC AS WALLPAPER

Fabric on walls does not hide imperfections. So why use fabric? For drama! A super look can be achieved by using the same pattern fabric on the walls that is in your drapes and, in the case of a bedroom, in your bedspread, as well. Fabric on the walls cannot be cleaned so it is not a good choice where soiling is inevitable, such as a kitchen or child's room. One of the benefits is that fabric adds a certain sheen to the walls that is missing in wallpaper. It's best to exper-

Hand stenciling can be just the finishing touch needed to bring together the color scheme of a room. In this room, the Colonial-style furniture is complemented by the traditional stencil design.

iment with this technique in a small room first or on just one wall of a room. It helps if you've had basic wallpapering experience, as well.

For your first project, I recommend using a fabric with a design, so that any slight irregularities or discolorations from the wall won't show through as readily as they would with a plain-colored fabric. Also, try to select fabric without a pattern so the pieces do not need to be matched horizontally. A pattern that has to be matched takes more fabric and is a little difficult to align since fabric stretches when dampened with wallpaper glue. For complete directions on applying a fabric wall covering, see pages 105 to 106 in Chapter 6.

STENCILING WALLS

Stenciling can add a lot to a room. The great thing about stenciling is that you can customize the colors used to perfectly pull the room's color scheme together. (See photo at left.) You can also get just the right amount of pattern on the walls. The imperfections in the intensity of the paint application and the pattern that result from hand stenciling give a charm that wallpaper cannot duplicate. An alternative to stenciling entire walls is stenciling trim around windows, doors, and so forth. You can also make matching curtains by applying the same stencils to fabric, using embroidery paint.

There are many books available on stenciling (see reading list on page 127). Do some reading, practice on a piece of cardboard, and then don't think twice about making that first brush stroke on the wall.

MURAL WALL PAINTING

It is not necessary to be a highly skilled artist to paint a wall mural. Murals are most frequently scenes and are often done in the folk-art style. Perspective is not required for this look (reminiscent of Grandma Moses). A mural is usually done on an entire wall or on the section of wall above a chair rail in a hallway, stair well, or dining room.

To design a mural, first do a small sketch on graph paper sized to scale in the same proportion as your wall. Once you have a design you like, transfer it to your wall in pencil and then begin painting, doing the largest, most important elements first.

This ½"–thick brick facing is so real-looking that even my home inspector was fooled.

Acrylic paints work fine for this type of project. You can use simple paint application techniques such as sponge dabbing to create many of the simple shapes and fill in long images such as tree branches. A contemporary design could easily be painted using straight lines, curves, and angles. Murals for a child's room can include animals, nursery characters, trains, boats, paper dolls — just tap the resources of your child's and your own imagination!

BRICK FACING

Brick facing is one of the most effective and realistic "fake" wall finishes you can use; it works best if you use real brick facing made of clay. This is like regular bricks; the only difference is the ½″ thickness. These bricks cost about 50¢ apiece. Corners (L-shaped pieces) cost about 90¢ each, but you don't usually need very many corners. The brick is applied with quick-set mortar, and once that is dry, grout is worked in between the bricks.

A wet saw is the best tool for cutting the bricks and can be rented. Another, slower, method is to score the bricks with a skill saw and then snap them. Undoubtedly you will have more waste with this method, however, since the brick often breaks unevenly.

How realistic does this brick facing look? After I finished my kitchen, I had it inspected by a professional home inspector because I intended to sell the house. I wanted to make sure I hadn't overlooked any potential problems. The inspector said, "Pauline, you did a good job except for one thing." I'm thinking, *Oh no!* Then he continued, "You didn't put in extra reinforcement to support the weight of the brick." Well, he couldn't have said anything more complimentary. My brick facing looked so real that he thought it was full bricks. I tried not to be smug when I told him the brick was only facing, but I'm still grinning.

PANELING WITH PINE BOARDS

Wide pine boards can be used to create a magnificent wall finish for a library or family room. This look works particularly well on a wall surrounding a fireplace, with bookshelves built in on either side. Before the boards are attached to the wall (with nails), have them beaded in a cabinet shop. Beading involves cutting a rounded groove that runs the entire length of each wide board. It is not expensive to have done.

Once the boards are in place on the wall, apply

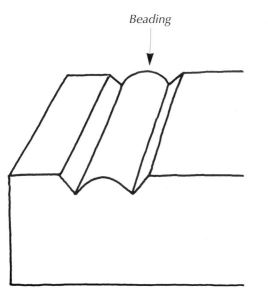

Beading

Pine boards can be beaded at a cabinetry shop in preparation for paneling.

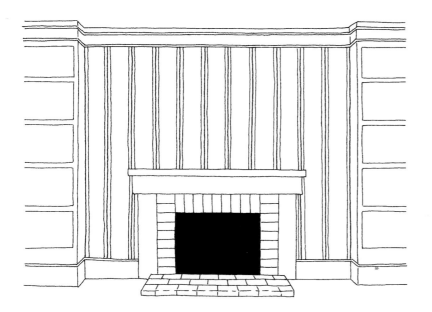

Wood paneling applied to a wall around a fireplace creates a great look for a library or family room.

moldings across the top of the boards, and continue around the entire perimeter of the room. If you have a fireplace, construct a mantel from the same pine boards. Then stain all the boards a rich shade of cherry and your room will feel stately.

Architectural Molding

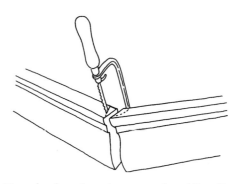

Architectural molding qualifies in that important category of "an architectural feature" — one of the design coordinates that promotes an easy flow throughout your home. Adding or beautifying moldings is one of the best values you can get for your decorating dollars. Moldings are:

- Relatively inexpensive
- Quick to install
- Helpful in covering up poor taping deficiencies (such as line cracks in the corners or uneven corners)
- Architectural accents

To make the mitered corners of molding fit precisely, use a coping saw to cut out the excess wood behind the angled corners before fitting them together.

I've found molding to be quite versatile in decorating. Although it is most commonly placed where the ceiling meets the walls, it can also be used on the wall over a fireplace to simulate raised paneling, to trim the perimeter of plain cupboard doors, to create a chair railing, to frame the perimeters of flush lauan (hollow) doors for a Shaker look, or around the outside of a mirror fastened flush on a wall.

Wood trim can add a decorative touch to other pieces in your home, as well. Small (1″) molding can be fastened to the horizontal edge of otherwise plain shelving. Molding can also be attached around the top of bookcases to make pieces more attractive. Kitchen cabinets will look custom made if you extend heavy molding from the top of the cabinets up to the ceiling (as shown in the "after" photo on page 57). Raised paneling can be simulated by making "frames" on the walls below a chair railing. The molding chosen for the squares should be flat on the back side and beveled toward the center.

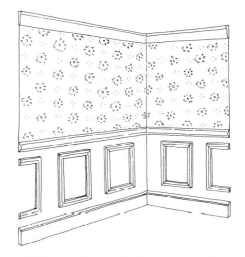

Molding can be applied to a plain wall to create a totally new look. A chair railing combined with square frames simulates the look of raised paneling.

Moldings are now available in a lightweight composite material that resembles plaster. All sizes and styles are available in this material, but it is more costly than wood moldings.

INSTALLING MOLDING

It takes a little practice to get the angles right, but you can learn to install molding yourself. If you don't feel confident about working with molding, you might consider taking a class in making frames first. Applying molding employs the same technique as frame-making, but on a larger scale. And just

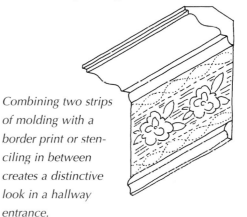

Combining two strips of molding with a border print or stenciling in between creates a distinctive look in a hallway entrance.

Ordinary plain kitchen cabinets can be transformed to striking Shaker-style cabinets with the addition of new birch plywood faces edged with pine molding.

think — you can save a lot of money making your own frames! Craft and art supply shops often offer framing classes.

In terms of equipment, you'll need a coping saw to cut off excess wood on the end cuts on the back side of the molding. This will make it easier to join the miter cut with the adjoining corner. You'll also need a fairly decent miter box, finishing nails, a nail set, a small hammer, a countersink punch, and a good tape measure.

Before cutting your actual molding pieces, practice cutting corner angles on scraps and see how they fit together. Cut off excess back material, place in position, and, presto, you have molding.

You should prime and paint all molding before installation and thereby avoid having to mask off the wall later to protect it while painting the molding. You will, however, need to do a little touching up around nail holes and corners on the installed molding.

CREATING A CUSTOM LOOK WITH MOLDING

For a custom kitchen look, mount a cupboard door on either end of an unpaneled side cabinet. Do this with either upper or lower cabinets. The cabinet doors are only decorative and are permanently fastened with glue and screws. It may be necessary to use more than one cabinet door to fill in a large space —

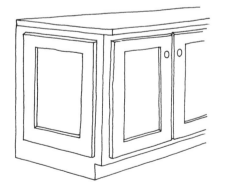

Mounting "fake" cupboard doors on the ends of side cabinets creates the detailed look of expensive custom cabinets.

Architectural molding was applied over this fireplace to simulate raised paneling. The slight shade variation in paint color between the "panel" and adjoining wall re-enforces the effect.

for example, the back side of an island. The detailing and elegance of this look are worth the investment in a few more doors!

A house I worked on recently had a kitchen in desperate need of remodeling. When I thought about what style would be most appropriate, it cried out *Shaker*. The Shaker style is rather simple; a wide plain molding lines the perimeter of each door. The width of the bottom stile is always deeper than the rest of the molding, which creates a look that is pleasing to the eye.

To replicate the Shaker look on the kitchen cabinets, I applied ⅜"-thick molding of clear pine over a birch plywood base. These strips are 2⅛" wide at the top and sides, and 2⅞" wide at the bottom of each cabinet door. I had a carpenter make new doors with simple 1¼" wooden knobs for the existing base cupboards, which were in good shape.

To carry the Shaker theme throughout the kitchen, I faced the flat refrigerator front with ¼" birch plywood (see box). I couldn't find a handle in the appropriate size, so the carpenter made one out of mahogany.

This custom-look refrigerator front was created from ¼" birch plywood!

Then I installed black appliances and finished the countertop with 12" white marbleized floor tile, which I continued up the wall to beneath the cupboards (not just the traditional 4" above the countertop). A 1" thick, 30" long, 6" high piece of stainless steel was cut in a curve and positioned over the double ovens to replicate the shape of the design of an original Shaker oven. (A metal fabrication shop will cut the stainless steel.) The built-in double ovens and microwave were recessed in an area that was faced with brick.

FACING THE REFRIGERATOR DOOR

A sheet of ¼" plywood can be fastened to the front of your refrigerator with short screws driven through from the inside of the door, just outside the gasket. If your gasket extends to the door edge, center the screw in the gasket itself. Screwing through the metal door does not impair the function of the refrigerator. Molding can then be glued to the front of the refrigerator door to cover the screws. (Another method for fastening the facing on lightweight metal is to use construction adhesive such as Liquid Nails.) Finish the look by staining or painting the surface. I installed cabinet doors above the refrigerator (pictured at left) to complete the custom-cabinet look.

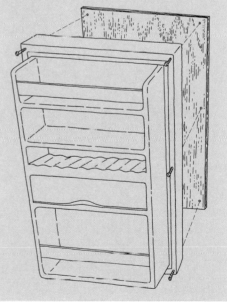

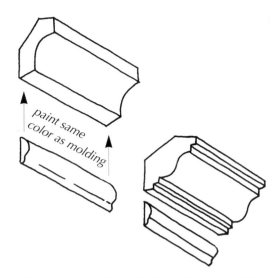

You can create the look of one impressive 5″ molding (above left) by applying a strip of 3″ crown molding to the top perimeter of a room and a flat strip of molding about 2″ below and then painting or staining the two strips and the wall area in between the same color.

Another technique for creating the look of an elegant molding (above right) is to combine two smaller moldings.

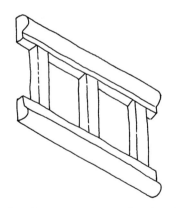

Rather than buying expensive dentil molding, you can make your own by glueing small pieces of wood between two strips of molding. This is very manageable for a small area.

Crown moldings, the type that can be angled into the corner around the perimeter of a ceiling, are slightly more difficult to install than molding that is simply placed on the wall next to the ceiling. Because they are installed angularly to the wall ceiling, added visual appeal results.

One of my favorite tricks to make molding look really impressive is to attach a simple crown molding approximately 2″ to 3″ thick to the upper perimeter of the room. Next, I attach a flat strip of molding in a compatible design to the wall about 2″ below the first molding, leaving a space in between. I paint or stain this space the same color as the two moldings. The result is what appears to be one large, impressive molding over 5″ thick.

The cost of this molding arrangement is quite manageable. Crown molding is approximately $2 per foot. The smaller flat molding is 40¢ per foot. For a room 12′ x 14′, the total cost is about $125.

To further enhance this molding trick, glue small painted pieces of wood between the two pieces of molding. This is called dentil molding. Cutting and applying the individual pieces would be a lengthy process for anything but a small area. However, this type of molding can be purchased preassembled, although it is fairly expensive. Whatever form you buy it in, dentil molding gives a room a classy, elegant look.

EFFECTS WITH CASINGS

The basic reason for casings is to provide a method of finishing the joints around windows, doors, and other architectural features. But why be basic? That is where decorative casing comes into play — the utilitarian can be dressed up by simply adding a bead (groove) or by placing a corner-round molding on top of a square-edged piece or by numerous other choices, such as:

- Most basic
- Slightly fancy
- Very fancy
- Standard in many homes today — clamshell molding, which is very narrow and very thin

A finish carpenter may have the routing bits that can duplicate a variety of casing styles. Colonial casings vary in the detailing but are not nearly as intricate as casings of the high style of the Victorian era. A good percentage of Victorian woodwork dating from the 1860s to the 1900s was constructed of oak and was originally varnished.

One noticeable difference between pre-1940s and contemporary casings is the size. Why aren't casings, baseboards, and moldings used the same way today as they were 100 years ago? There is one easy answer: Cost! I cannot begin to imagine how much it would cost to duplicate high-quality, authentic Victorian woodwork today. The amount would be staggering.

Doors

Lauan doors are unpaneled, hollow-core, inexpensive doors found in many houses. In the house I decorated with a Shaker-style look, I transformed several of the hallway doors opening into the kitchen to be consistent with the rest of the house. To accomplish this, I used ⅜″–thick pine facing to create the look of cabinetry molding, with 3½″–wide strips on the top, sides, and middle and 5″–wide strips along the bottom (the same design used on my kitchen cupboards, page 44). The resulting look is truly Shaker.

Next to the hall is a bedroom that I decided to carry the Shaker theme into as well. This room included a wall of closets with very utilitarian-looking, lauan doors. First, I faced each of the four doors off with ⅜″–wide pine molding, as described in the previous section for individual doors. One of the challenges was to accommodate the extra depth the molding created on each of the sliding doors. To make it easier for the modified doors to slide past each other, I removed the metal bracket that holds the doors along the top frame of the doorway and took it to a metal fabricator shop, where they cut it in half lengthwise. Then I reattached the two strips of bracket to the frame, far enough away from each other to accommodate the extra depth of the molding.

Next, I made the Sheetrock wall above the sliding doors look like cupboard doors by applying fake fronts — cupboard doors nailed directly to the Sheetrock. The doors are edged with ½″ pine facing which I applied around the vertical members of the door frame as well to create the look of a built-in unit. The detailing on the fake doors includes hinges and wooden knobs.

To finish off the look, I attached Shaker-style peg handles to each sliding door by drilling and then gluing small-diameter screws through the back side. I then painted the entire wall of closets and fake cupboards a wedgewood blue color, creating a gorgeous focal point for the room. (See photo on next page.)

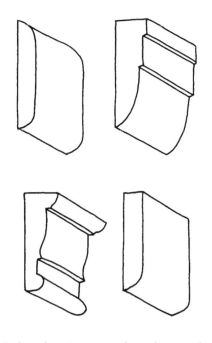

Styles of casings range from the most basic (top left) to the more detailed. Clamshell molding (bottom right) tends to be one of the least interesting, and most prevalent, styles of molding used in many modern homes.

MODIFYING LAUAN DOORS

Applying molding to lauan doors can create the look of more expensive doors. It's quite simple to do, with the following steps:

1. Remove the door from its hinges. Remove the hinges and doorknobs from the door.
2. Apply ⅜″ molding around the perimeter of the door and through the middle. Apply in the same manner as described on page 44 for kitchen cupboards.
3. Reattach the hinges and doorknobs. It is necessary to move the hinges. The doorknobs are a little tricky because not much of the threaded shank is left to screw on from one side to the other. If the molding is any thicker than ⅜″, different door knobs will be necessary.

An English-cottage style (left) and southwestern style (right) are two of the many patterns that can be created.

Before molding is applied to plain Lauan doors, the metal bracket that holds the sliding doors has to be removed, split through the center, and reinstalled to allow for additional thickness of doors with molding. The ⅜" thick pine molding is glued to the doors and attached with finishing nails. Fake built-in overhead cupboards can be made by affixing doors edged all around with ½" pine facing. The facing here extends down the vertical lines of the doors as well, to create a built-in look.

Before alterations

Applying molding

Ordinary-looking sliding closet doors can be modified to look like traditional Shaker doors with the application of moldings, peg handles, and (fake) overhead cabinets.

Wood Flooring

In recent years, wood flooring has again become the flooring of choice. There are three main reasons for its resurgent popularity.

1. **Appearance.** Wood floors are good-looking. Whether finished with a low-satin sheen or a highly polished glow, the grains of the wood show through to produce an interesting, non-manufactured look. Wood stains, which are available in an unlimited variety of colors, enhance the overall look. The warmth of a stain in provincial pine can be a critical component of the country colonial look. A dark mahogany stain adds a deeper, more elegant tone to a room. The color tone of a wood floor contributes substantially to defining a look.

2. **Air quality.** A major concern in the 1990s is the quality of air indoors. Since 80 to 85 percent of our time is spent inside, it is a high priority to use building and decorating materials that are less likely to promote the growth of bacteria. Under certain circumstances, carpeting can become a breeding ground for bacteria. After only 3 hours on a damp carpet, bacteria can multiply from 2 to 18 million in 24 hours. Dust mite feces as well as the bacteria attach themselves to any dust particles 3 microns or larger. This is not a great environment for allergy-sufferers! It is much easier to thoroughly clean wood floors than carpeted areas.

3. **Cleaning.** Wood floors are easy to clean by damp-mopping if they have been finished with several coats of protective coating. Polyurethane is by far the most popular finish. Wood floors can be forgiving; if you nick or scratch them, a little stain and the damage is blended and is no longer noticeable.

If your house has wall-to-wall carpeting and you would prefer wood flooring, you can consider a number of options, depending on the general look you are trying to achieve. These include:

■ Oak flooring in narrow (3"–4") widths
■ Cherry flooring in 4"–6" widths
■ Fir flooring, which resembles oak
■ Yellow pine, which is moderately hard
■ Native pine, which is fairly soft but is available in very wide boards, 10"–12" and sometimes wider
■ Prefinished narrow widths of oak (one of the newest products available)

PROS AND CONS OF WIDE PINE FLOORBOARDS

Pros:

■ Old country look (although they would also look super with contemporary)
■ Floor goes down quickly
■ Easy installation job for do-it-yourselfer
■ Very reasonable cost
■ Takes stain easily
■ Hand sanding is not difficult
■ Gets antiqued, worn look quickly
■ You can use cut nails (available at lumber stores), which look like old square-headed nails

Cons:

■ Pine is soft, and dents and mars easily (this bothers some people)
■ Wide pine boards will shrink, creating spaces between the boards (The size of the cracks varies with the seasons — the boards shrink in the low humidity of winter and swell in the summer. The wider the boards, the more expansion and contraction.)

STAINING WOOD FLOORS

There are many different ways to stain wood floors. Hardwood floors may be left natural or stained quite dark and all the shades in between. Some stains tend to have yellow casts like blond hair, while others tend more toward gray, like ash-gray hair. Cherry tones are decidedly red. Pine floors can be stained vibrant colors such as grass green, wedgewood blue, and pickled white. Your imagination is the only limit. To make your decision, go back to the decorating reference materials you have assembled (see Chapter 1) and analyze the color photos you selected to identify what appeals to you and will enhance the look of your rooms.

PINE FLOORING

There are two basic types of pine flooring: soft and hard. Hard pine is not as readily available as soft. It is much more costly, and the wider widths are difficult to come by. Soft pine is available through local lumber companies in 12″ widths. You can buy 1″x12″ #2 pine from 8′ to 16′ lengths. It usually comes planed on both sides and square edged, ready to install. The thickness of the boards is approximately ¾″. Some home owners prefer the pine boards to be tongue and grooved. If you want wider widths, go to a lumber mill and ask for the widest pine they have. It comes in random widths (my last batch varied from 10″–17″).

Buckling may be a problem. If boards are too dry and the floor is laid too tightly, the boards will swell and buckle in the summer. This condition is more apt to occur with hardwoods that are very low in moisture content and are laid in the winter. Even kiln-dried lumber may pick up moisture in the time it is hauled to the lumber company, stored in an unheated room, and then transported to your house. You can keep shrinkage to a minimum by testing the moisture content of the lumber before installation. To do this you'll need a moisture meter, which costs about $100 (you might be able to rent one). Recommended readings are 7 to 8 percent. Before laying a floor, test the boards for moisture content. If the reading is above 8 percent, you should season the boards until they are drier and meet the desired reading.

Seasoning is best done right inside your house. Stack the lumber in layers, perpendicular to each other, with small sticks between each layer. Maintain a temperature of 65° to 70°F for a minimum of three weeks; four to six weeks is preferable. If you jump the gun and put the floor down earlier, you may end up with wider crevices between boards than necessary.

Sanding hardwood (oak) floors to remove old varnish is one job I like to leave to the professionals. As a woman, I find the heavy sanding machine difficult to hang on to. If your budget allows, hire someone to do the job; if you need to save money, you can rent the necessary equipment and do it yourself. For instructions on refinishing wide board pine floors, see pages 117 to 119.

Other Floor Coverings

While wood is probably the most versatile floor covering, there are other coverings that work well in particular situations. As you think about the functions of various areas of your house, and the types of activities and use that occur there, you may find that a particular floor covering best helps ease the noise or keeps the dirt and dust under control.

CARPET

Carpeting holds a prominent place in decorating. It can cover a multitude of sins and unify all areas of the house. The color choices are fabulous and the texture choices almost unlimited. Carpeting can range in price from several dollars a square yard to an average of $15 to $25 per yard. For real savings, purchase remnants for small areas. Most carpet stores have a remnant section.

The weight of the carpet, determined by the density of the material, is one factor to consider when comparison shopping. The heavier the weight the denser the pile usually is. Padding is important, too. An otherwise mediocre carpet will look and feel plush if a high-quality padding is installed underneath.

Installation of carpeting on a large scale is better left to the professionals unless you do some research and learn a few tricks, such as how to seam the carpet from the back side, how to lay down the tack strip, and how to use the knee kicker to stretch out the carpet so wrinkles don't develop.

I've used carpeting successfully in well-ventilated bathrooms, where it has lasted anywhere from one to three years with everyday wear. (Definitely seek out sale remnants for this use.) If you decide on wall-to-wall carpeting in a bathroom you will likely install it yourself. Cutting around all those objects in such a small space is tricky. I've found the best way to work is to first make a pattern with heavy paper. Getting around the toilet is the hardest part, and it may take a couple of tries to get the pattern right. I recommend making one straight cut behind the toilet to get around the bowl area. Work from one corner to the toilet first before you do the rest of the room. Try taping down the paper pattern to hold it in place. Always mark the side of the paper facing you **"Right Side Up"** in bold letters. When you cut the carpet, put the right side of the pattern pieces against the wrong side of the carpeting. If you don't, the carpet pieces will be backward. Cut the carpet on the wrong side, using a razor. Have plenty of blades on hand, since they will dull quickly. When the carpet is laid the cut edges will come together and not be noticeable.

TILE AND LINOLEUM

These are very durable flooring materials that last for years. Sheet linoleum was installed in my hair-styling salon over thirty years ago. Even with all the

Courtesy of Pergo flooring

This look-alike wood flooring offers the beauty of wood with more stability and less initial preparation work then the real thing.

wear and tear of salon products and heavy traffic, the marbled white floor looks beautiful today.

Inexpensive adhesive-backed tiles are a good choice for the short term (a few years) or for light-traffic areas. They look good and are very easy to install. With scissors you can trim tiles where necessary. They're a perfect solution for unattractive floors in a rented apartment.

BRICK

Full brick blocks, brick pavers (about half the thickness), or brick facing (½" thick) are all great flooring choices for entryways or mud rooms. As feet pass over bricks, dirt is trapped in the grouted crevices and doesn't get tracked through the rest of the house. Sealer can be applied to brings out the brick color and repeal wetness.

Brick facing is an easy do-it-yourself project. The bricks — like the wall facing discussed on page 42 — are set in mastic or quick-set mortar. When dry, grout is placed in the space between bricks and indented slightly. A wet saw works best for cutting the facing.

Brick pavers and full brick are an option if you have the depth to make them level with your existing floor. Laying bricks is not hard but it is time-consuming and messy work for the amateur.

There is no more practical floor for an entranceway than brick. It lasts forever, stands up under rain and snow, and repels most stains. Slate is another good choice for a water-resistant surface. It can be laid in an irregular-edged or square-edged style. However, slate tends to be more slippery when wet than brick.

MATERIALS THAT LOOK LIKE TRADITIONAL WOOD FLOORING

Engineered look-alike wood flooring is fairly new to our market, and although I haven't tried it yet, I've heard positive reviews from many people who have. The flooring comes prefinished with a multilayered, permanently hardened finish. One major benefit is that the extra time and inconvenience of finishing a new wood floor are eliminated.

This flooring, made up of three layers of material bonded with adhesive under extreme heat and pressure, is reputed to be 75 percent more stable than solid wood flooring. The resulting tongue-and-groove boards will withstand two professional refinishing jobs. This flooring is available in a variety of wood types, and can be used with a radiant heating system.

Chapter 4

Transforming Your Home Room by Room

The Top 10 Features

The "Top 10" lists used by a popular TV talk-show host are the perfect way to describe the elements that make a room really special. I've made up a list of the top 10 features for each room in the house, based on my experience of buying or building, remodeling, and then reselling different houses over the past several years. These features include both decorating and remodeling components, since the two go hand-in-hand.

You may find these lists particularly helpful if you are remodeling or looking for a house to buy. They go beyond the obvious features (such as good-quality appliances in the kitchen) to include what really gives a house that little bonus that makes it stand out from others in terms of both function and beauty.

The Top 10 Kitchen Features

The kitchen is the most used and remodeled room in the house. In this age of two working spouses and long working hours, an outdated kitchen means wasted time and ruined dispositions.

Window Space Over the Sink

Problem: Kitchen designs always feature big windows over the sink, but doesn't this cut down on the space in your upper cabinets?

Solution: I, too, have noticed many kitchens featured in magazines with extended windows over the sink. There's a trade-off here, however. If your dishwasher is next to the sink, you need cupboard space directly above for dishes. Otherwise, unloading the dishes becomes inconvenient and inefficient. So, be cautious about putting too large a window in; I'd opt for the cabinet space over an extended window space.

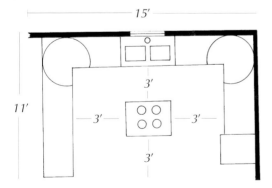

A kitchen island requires 3' of space on all sides to allow for easy movement around it.

1 Pantry. As far as pantries go, the bigger, the better. If you don't have a separate laundry room include enough space for a washer and dryer, fold-down ironing board, and chutes for returnable bottles and recyclables (if you have a basement in which you can keep barrels to catch them). It's important that the pantry be located very near the working area (stove, sink, and refrigerator). Line the pantry walls with lots of shelves designed to meet your personal height requirements.

Building a pantry can save you money, since it is much less expensive to build a "miniroom" than to purchase the equivalent finished kitchen cabinets.

2 Drawer space. It's almost impossible to have too many drawers. Ten to twelve, 4"–6" deep, will hold all the aluminum foil, spatulas, dish towels, and packaged gravy mix you'll ever need.

3 Attractive, convenient appliances. I can't live without a microwave, but it must be built in. Otherwise it takes up valuable counter space. Over the stove is a good place to build in the unit if it would be too difficult to put it anywhere else. Microwave units for exactly that purpose are available with a light for the cooking surface below as well as a charcoal filter unit for venting.

A self-cleaning oven is another must for a busy kitchen. (Don't confuse "self-cleaning" with "continuous cleaning." Continuous-cleaning ovens do not work as well as self-cleaning ones.)

4 Island. Islands are useful for various purposes. Some serve as simply additional counter space, while others feature a butcher-block counter. Sinks and stoves are sometimes built into islands. An island should have 3' of space around it, so the kitchen should be at least 11'x15' to accommodate it.

5 Wood paneling on refrigerator. Maybe you'll miss hanging all those messy papers and notes all over the refrigerator, but why not beautify it (and your kitchen) by treating it like another cabinet? Why not put all those important papers on a bulletin board in or near the kitchen? With some refrigerators (and dishwashers) on the market, you can buy thin wood panels that attach to the front, or you can make them yourself (see page 45).

6 Large, deep sink (with a tall faucet and a sprayer). If you have a dishwasher, you don't need a double sink. Instead, one large, deep sink (approximately 21" wide by 32" long by 9" deep) is sufficient. Less water splashes out of the sink, and you can get any pot under the tall curved spigot. The sprayer works very well for rinsing out the sink, washing your hair, and bathing the baby.

7 Backsplash surface on wall above countertop. Typically, a short (4") backsplash is installed perpendicular to the countertop. Extending this surface so it runs up the wall to meet the upper cupboards looks good and functions better than the shorter version. Decorative tile is a great touch if you have Formica countertops. Or you can use the same formica on the backsplash as on the countertop, in a color you love.

8 Eating bar. An eating bar is very useful, providing a place to eat alone, for visitors to hang out, or for serving a buffet. I highly recommend building one, even if your dining table is nearby.

If you build an eating bar on the "backside" of an existing counter, the bar surface should be about 6″ higher than the counter. The additional height hides some of the cooking surface from view and will accommodate electrical outlets installed horizontally. Many electrical codes require outlets every 2′ of counter space.

9 Good artificial light. Recessed lighting (canister type) is unobtrusive. Five to seven of these lights will illuminate a medium-sized kitchen very effectively. Installation requires new wiring. If this isn't possible, another option is very shallow fluorescent fixtures (about 3″ deep) that hold two round tubes and put out tremendous light. The cover is plain, so the fixture is inconspicuous.

BUILDING AN EATING BAR

You can construct your own inexpensive, yet substantial-looking, eating bar by taking the following steps.

1. Glue together (with carpenter's wood glue) two 1″x10″ pine boards (one on top of the other). Once this piece is solidly glued, edge all four sides of it with 2″ wide x 1½″ deep bread-board strips of pine. (These solid strips of wood can be cut from a basic 2x4 pine stud.) The edging covers the seam and makes the bar look like one 2″–thick piece of wood.

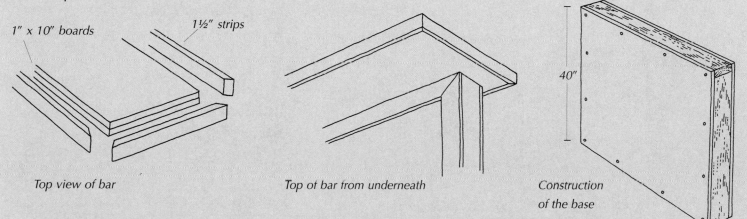

1″ x 10″ boards *1½″ strips*

Top view of bar *Top of bar from underneath* *Construction of the base* *40″*

2. You will need a 40″–high half-wall for mounting the bar. This half-wall can be constructed from scratch of 2x4 wood assembled in the configuration of a rather shallow rectangle and covered with Sheetrock (see illustration), or it can be cut down from an existing room wall. Before cutting, be sure to ask a professional if the existing room wall is a load-bearing wall. A room can still be opened up if this situation exists but additional reinforcement in the ceiling may be necessary — a job to be done by a professional carpenter. If you need this work it will take, at most, two days for a carpenter to install paralams or other heavy duty reinforcement. Some states require a qualified civil engineer to calculate the size of any additional reinforcement needed.

3. Use wood screws and carpenter's construction glue to fasten the top to the base.

This eating bar top was made from two 1"x10" pine boards (see instructions on previous page) mounted on a half-wall. Note that the baseboard heating was enclosed to create a footrest.

10 **Skylight.** Since you spend a lot of time in the kitchen, light is essential. If a skylight is possible above the work area (and especially if the roof needs redoing anyway), it's worth making the small investment to install one. I have had skylight windows that open as well as those that stay closed (stationary), and find the stationary type just fine. If you have a motorized opener you would no doubt use it, but otherwise skylights are generally awkward to open.

In one of my kitchens I positioned a skylight over the stove in the island. The skylight itself wasn't particularly large, so the well was extended on the sides to line up with the island below. This visually enlarges the skylight and directs light onto the stove.

If it is not structurally feasible or you do not want to invest in a skylight, try letting in more light by putting in two windows next to each other or one extra wide window centered over the sink.

The light from this small skylight was extended over a larger area by opening up the angles of the window well.

Quick Decorating Tips for Kitchens

If you're on a tight budget, here are some options for replacing or rejuvenating old-looking kitchen cupboards, walls, trim, floors, and countertops.

CUPBOARDS

✔ If the cupboards are structurally sound, replace and/or refinish the doors. Doors can be purchased at home improvement supply stores, although the available sizes are generally limited.

✔ Replace all cupboards with the prefab type, which you buy unassembled and put together yourself. Home supply stores carry them. But compare the price of unassembled and preassembled cupboards first.

✔ Buy finished cabinets. Be sure to do some comparative shoping, since the price for the same item can vary greatly. Wait for sales if you can.

✔ Ask at specialty kitchen shops if they have any model setups for sale (floor models are usually cheaper). Or check the "Articles for Sale" column in your local paper or Want Ad Digest for good buys.

✔ If wood-stained cabinets are worn around the handles, touch them up with ZAR stain. If you're not sure what color stain will match, remove one of the cabinet doors and take it with you to the paint store. Then ask the clerk what product and color is suitable for a small touch-up on that surface. Keep in mind that touching up worn spots won't bring back the shiny finish. You may have to polyurethane the entire door. In the case of painted cabinet doors that need touching up, you can sand and repaint, or use an antiquing kit.

✔ If unpaneled cabinet doors are worn around the handles, cover up the worn area by painting a 2″ to 3″ molding around the perimeter of the door. Sometimes just a good polish with Old English Polish & Scratch Remover is all that is necessary.

✔ To create a new look on flush solid wood cabinets with a worn finish, begin by sanding the finish off the doors and drawers. Then take these pieces to a cabinet shop and have a ½″–wide line routed approximately 2″ in from the edges. This detail adds a smart look to otherwise plain door fronts. Sand down the casings and then pickle or paint the casings, doors, and drawers.

WALLS AND TRIM

✔ If walls need to be painted, choose a color that will make the kitchen look bright. Color-coordinate walls and cupboards. If the walls are not in good shape, cover them with a durable, patterned vinyl wallpaper.

BEFORE

AFTER

The cupboards in this kitchen were transformed by a new, light paint job. The counters were recovered with white tile, which was extended up to the bottom of the cabinets, making a good high backsplash surface.

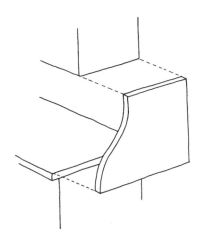

To create a finished look on the ends of your kitchen cabinets:

1. Fill in the space between the cabinets and the counter with side panels.

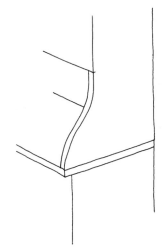

2. Paint the cabinets and panels the same color as your countertop Formica for the effect of a very large cupboard.

FLOORS

✔ If there are hardwood floors under the old linoleum, remove the linoleum.

✔ If an asphalt tile floor is in bad shape, place self-adhering tile over it.

✔ If your wooden floors are in poor shape and you do not want to go to the expense or inconvenience of sanding, try using one coat of poly/stain (a colored polyurethane). This product will sometimes blend worn spots.

COUNTERS

✔ Coordinate countertops with other kitchen features. The toughest colors to deal with are the very bold ones that were popular a number of years ago, like orange or bright blue or avocado. If you are dealing with tones like these, try to work them into a color scheme that repeats these tones in wallpaper, accessories, stenciling, and fabric. Fiesta Ware dishes, with their strong colors, would work well on a dish rack.

✔ Try paneling or painting dishwashers and refrigerators whose colors are outdated. I've successfully painted appliances. To do this, sand the appliance lightly first, then apply enamel automobile paint. Mask off chrome parts and protect everything around the appliance if spraying inside the house. You have to be careful afterward with abrasive cleaners, but you can touch up paint as time goes on.

✔ If your kitchen features an island, you can create an elegant look by covering the island countertop in real granite and using Formica that looks like granite on the rest of the counters. The eye focuses on the island, and the overall effect is that it's all the real thing.

✔ If you have a cabinet overhang or nook, try installing a food warmer light. I borrowed this idea from pictures I saw of a million-dollar house outside of San Diego. I just use a simple swing-arm lamp with a 250-watt infrared bulb and it works great.

Top 10 Dining Area Features

There is nothing like a lovely dining area that is conducive to both lively family mealtime conversation and larger, more formal dinners. This more versatile use of the same space is supplanting the old distinction between formal and informal dining rooms. If you have an area convenient to the kitchen that is used daily for meals, why not make that space attractive and sizable enough to serve all your meals in? A dining room used twice a year is not an efficient allocation of space.

1 **Space for a table to accommodate four to sixteen people.** It's great to have the space to handle a table that will accommodate a large sit-down dinner when needed. If the room is large enough, the table can be lengthened with leaves or by adding card tables with a plywood extension on top cut to the same width as the table. To match the height of the table, put books and magazines under the plywood and cover with a floor-length tablecloth.

2 Light fixture (chandelier type) that can be hooked in any direction. Purchase a chandelier with a chain at least 20″ long, which will allow you to hang the chandelier wherever you need to while leaving the electrical ceiling connection stationary. Attach the fixture with an eye hook screwed into the ceiling.

3 Built-in dish cupboard or space for cupboard. Why not display and enjoy the beauty of your best china or decorative dinnerware? One way to make sure you can display it easily is to develop a color scheme for the room based on your china pattern.

4 Proximity to kitchen. If the dining table is used all the time, it is important that it be close to the kitchen, preferably within 15′ to 20′ of the kitchen sink. Otherwise you are walking many extra steps.

5 Easy access from the living room. After dinner, it's nice to have an easy flow of traffic into the living room, particularly when you have guests. If rooms open into each other, it seems less stuffy and stilted to "move" guests between rooms. If some of the party lingers around the dinner table and others are in the living room, the party seems more cohesive if rooms are not "down the hallway."

6 View of the outdoors. Not everyone has a view of Mount Shasta or the Pacific Ocean. So create a scene outside worthy of viewing. Even if you have a tiny space, you can design a garden to add beauty and peace to your meals (with the help of a few good gardening books). Aren't the prized tables at many fine restaurants positioned in front of a window with a view? Duplicate that experience for yourself.

7 Area that receives morning light. Nothing is more pleasant than having your morning coffee as you watch the sun rise or on a cold morning feeling the warmth of the sun's rays as you read the newspaper. If the house is sited so that the dining area receives sunlight into midday, so much the better. Dinner is usually too late or dark for sunshine anyhow, so wake up and look out at the weather while you have breakfast — you'll know how to dress for the day.

8 Architectural moldings. Architectural detailing makes a room feel special and important. The common rooms that are used most are, of course, seen most. Ceiling moldings, a chair railing, and simulated paneling beneath the chair railing dress up these rooms (see page 43). A contemporary feeling can be enhanced with large murals, horizontal stripes, or a fabric border finished off with a small piece of quarter-round molding.

9 Speakers hooked up to stereo system. Soft background music is pleasant at mealtimes. Some speakers are less than 10″ square, so they can easily be hidden behind a plant or chair or built into a wall. You can blend the speaker with

---

QUICK DECORATING TIPS FOR DINING ROOMS

✔ Make a floor-length tablecloth with a ruffle on the bottom and matching seat cushions that coordinate with any window treatments.

✔ If privacy isn't an issue, remove curtains completely and put up a simple valance or leave the windows unadorned.

✔ Put fresh flowers on the table. (The bouquet needn't be expensive — three daisies and some greens are quite charming.)

the walls by replacing the fabric face with a fabric the same color as the wall or dyeing a fabric like burlap to match.

10 **Closet in dining room to store linens.** If you have a closet in your dining room, try outfitting part of it with a wooden dowel rack to hang tablecloths. This saves ironing time, and helps you avoid searching for linens in the back of deep drawers.

Top 10 Family Room Features

Not only do folks want to look at a fireplace, they want to watch TV at the same time. The family room should be laid out so that it accommodates the variety of purposes family members use it for.

This built-in entertainment cabinet, holding a 32" TV, was built in at an angle to separate the home office space from the TV-watching area.

1 Built-in entertainment center. A good built-in should hold at least a 32″ TV in a cabinet that has doors and is high enough so that everyone can see.

2 Speakers hooked up to a built-in stereo system. These should be positioned for optimum sound and balance.

3 Charming architectural elements. The room should feel cozy and pleasant to be in. Architectural elements such as beams or fireplace detailing add to this homey quality.

4 Built-in bookcases. Measure your books and build shelves especially to accommodate them. If you have lots of small paperbacks, the shelves can be close together. But if you have many oversize books or photo albums, you will want shelves allowing 12″–14″ clearance or more.

5 Storage area for games. Allocate some closet cupboard space near the television or in a case piece of furniture to store playing cards, jigsaw puzzles, board games, and so forth. If the effort to find "fun" stuff is too hard, it's easy to give up on looking for it.

6 A comfortable and practical sofa. Cover the sofa in a sturdy fabric that can take abuse. Durability is the criterion for other upholstered pieces that are used daily as well. Patterns or medium-toned colors show soil the least.

7 Desk for home use.

8 Area for a computer. I suggest a neat hideaway arrangement contained in a 6′ closet with swing-out doors. Or find a roll-away table that fits neatly into a closet with louvered doors.

9 Location away from bedrooms. The noise of the television, stereo systems, or loud conversation won't wake up the children.

10 Fireplace. There is nothing like the ambience of an open flame flickering on a cool evening. Every home should have one. The installation of a fireplace is one investment which you should at least break even on when selling (provided it is the only fireplace in the house). If you don't have a fireplace already in place, there are several options for constructing one.

Masonry fireplace. In new construction a chimney can go on the inside or outside of the house. On the inside the masonry is less expensive because the flue can be constructed of cinder blocks. An interior chimney takes up considerable floor space. If brick or stone is used on an outside wall the cost is higher because of the cost of the additional material and the labor. Masonry fireplaces are the most expensive kind available, although prices vary considerably depending on the material and labor involved.

Zero-clearance fireplace. For an existing house with very limited space, this is a possibility, although a costly one if the installation is in a two-story house on an interior wall which requires insulated pipe. The firebox unit can be built in to look like a regular masonry fireplace — mantel and all!

Woodburning stove. If wood is being burned for the sole purpose of saving money on fuel, I recommend a woodburning furnace in the basement. Woodburning/oil furnace combinations are excellent in that the oil backup

QUICK DECORATING TIPS FOR FAMILY ROOMS

✔ Hide the TV in a cabinet that is as deep as the TV. If the depth misses by a few inches, cut a hole in the back of the cabinet. It won't show when placed against a wall. You can pull the plug through the hole, as well.

✔ Arrange your entertainment center neatly and attractively. If necessary, purchase book shelves for both books and electronic components.

✔ Use fabric for window treatments that coordinates with the slipcover on the sofa.

✔ If wall-to-wall carpets are stained or worn, place area rugs on top.

✔ Purchase a new coffee table if the one you have doesn't work in the decorating plan, or paint the one you have in an accent color.

✔ Group family photos on one wall.

✔ Find an exceptional accent piece for the wall and echo the color in the throw pillows.

kicks in if the wood burns up while you're away. Although I love a fireplace, continuous reliance on a wood stove as the primary source of heat poses a real challenge to keeping the house clean. (I lived with a woodburning stove for years.) There are some great-looking and efficient stoves (e.g., Vermont Castings), and they are your answer if a wood stove is what you want.

Gas fireplace. Boy, have these gotten good! If you have to purchase firewood and you're not into splitting logs, this could well be the way to go, especially if you use natural gas or you already have a propane tank. You simply push a button when you want a fire — no fuss, no muss! In fact, you can get a remote control like the one you have for the television. Gas fireplaces produce quite a lot of heat, so they're as cozy and satisfying as a woodburning fireplace. What makes these units so user friendly is that you no longer need a flue. The units are directly vented to the outside making them much less expensive than masonry fireplaces. Gas fireplaces can have a wood mantel and look as authentic as masonry ones.

Top 10 Library Features

Library rooms that offer quiet and escape from the TV and other activity are gaining popularity. Bookcases are rarely more than 12″ deep, so they don't take up much floor space. How many books constitute a library area? As few or as many as you like. An infrequently used room, such as a formal living room or dining room, can serve both its original purpose and that of a personal library.

It is unlikely that all of the top ten features of a library can be included in a dual-use room, but certain features are critical: bookcases, at least one easy chair, and a table lamp. It may take some shifting of furniture to fit in the books, but be creative.

If you're using a dining room, try mixing books and china in a large cabinet. Put the buffet in another room and build bookcases floor to ceiling in the buffet's place. To accommodate library space in a formal living room, remove your least-favorite overstuffed chair or an extra side table or console television and fill the resulting space with the widest-possible bookshelf.

1 Fireplace.
2 Shelves. You'll need lots of shelves sized to accommodate the height of your books. Any bookshelf longer than 4′ should have a vertical support in the middle.
3 Dictionary shelf. Construct a special deep shelf to hold an unabridged dictionary. Position the dictionary on a lazy-Susan bookstand — you'll use it more often.
4 Desk.
5 Comfortable reading chair.
6 Table lamps. These should be tall enough to cast good light over your favorite reading chair.

7 Attractive woodwork. Wood-tone woodwork enhances the library atmosphere. Wooden wall paneling adds even more (see page 42).

8 Excellent daylight. If you have the opportunity to read during the day, it's lovely to have sunlight streaming in. If you need window coverings for privacy, use a traverse rod so that opening the drapes isn't a hassle. If the room tends to be dark, enlarge an existing small window, especially if it's the only window in the room. Besides adding brightness, this will make the room seem larger.

9 Location away from the entertainment center.

10 Footstools. Place in front of each chair in the room.

Top 10 Master Bedroom Features

The master bedroom is that special space for you alone, a getaway. Some people prefer to have this retreat on the first floor to accommodate medical problems that may arise in the future that prevent climbing stairs; however, because of the square footage involved, it is often not financially practical. First-floor bedrooms take up a substantial portion of the whole first floor living area. The optimum bedroom size for the 10 desirable features listed here is approximately 400 square feet. If you were building a 2400-square-foot two-story house (40′ wide by 30′ deep) and wanted a master bedroom with these features on the first floor, it would take up one-third of the ground floor space.

I did not include a fireplace on my list for the master bedroom because, while it is marvelous for decorating, I find it too warm and seldom used.

1 Walk-in closet. The ideal walk-in closet is at least 6′ wide and 7′ deep. Wall space should be divided with racks or shelves from floor to ceiling. Allocate most of the wall space so that one rod is approximately 6′ high and another rod below it is 3′ high thus doubling the amount of rod space. The most efficient configuration is to have clothes racks along both sides and shelving in the back. Keep a short fold-up stepladder in the closet to reach shelves that are too high for you. Include shelves for shoes, which can comfortably be just 6″ apart (not including the thickness of the shelving). Shoes should be placed on the shelf with one shoe on top of the other, facing in opposite directions. Boots can be hung from a ½″ wooden rod with clothespins.

Outfitting a closet is a great do-it-yourself project. Metal brackets, fastened with molly screws into wall studs, are available in lumber stores to hold up the pole and support the shelves. Although the brackets are strong, I suggest that, if the shelf span is greater than 4′, three brackets be used, since clothes are heavy. Use either metal racks or 1″ thick by 12″ wide pine boards for shelving — this is a personal choice. I do not paint pine board shelves because after a couple of years they acquire a natural patina. Moreover, the rubbing of clothes hangers on painted rods wears off the paint.

QUICK DECORATING TIPS FOR BEDROOMS

✔ Avoid accumulating visible piles of books, newspapers, and magazines in the bedroom. Invest in an unfinished book case or shelves if necessary.

✔ Try grouping several small mirrors in nice frames over a chest of drawers.

✔ Rearrange the furniture to visually enlarge the space. Consider moving a piece of furniture from one bedroom to another if it works better in the second room.

✔ Add a wallpaper border next to the ceiling for a little drama. A hanging plant always looks nice in a bedroom.

✔ Repeat an accent color in a couple of different places, such as a lamp base, lampshade, bulletin board, or picture frame.

✔ Think about the arrangement of things on the walls and make a conscious decision about how to group them. Posters look neater if they are grouped together as a focal point. Smaller objects such as photos appear important if placed on a bulletin board or framed.

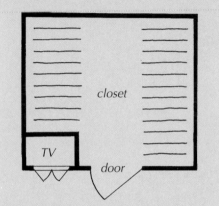

2   Room size of at least 12' x 18'. This is a size room that is one half again as large as a typical 12'x12' bedroom. The extra space can accommodate a sitting area and still have the feeling of spaciousness.

3   Wood floors. As with the rest of the house, wood floors are currently a popular choice and accommodate all kinds of area rug styles.

4   Outside entrance to balcony, deck, or patio. Having a bedroom with its own private outside entrance is classy and fun. Psychologically it's a step ahead of bedrooms that are "dead ends." For doors, I recommend French doors or sliders that are at least 6' wide. These full-view doors visually expand the room, making it appear larger than it actually is.

5   Speakers hooked up to stereo system. Bedroom speakers that are hooked up to the stereo system set up in the entertainment area in the family/great room make it easy to go from room to room without missing the music.

6   Television and phone hookups.

7   Heavy Drapes. Install drapes that are heavy enough to keep the room dim for a late-morning snooze.

8   Upholstered reading chair.

9   Private bathroom.

10 Location away from other bedrooms.

An entrance to an outdoor deck off the master bedroom enhances the spacious feeling of the room.

The Top 10 Bathroom Features

Because bathrooms are repeatedly used day and night, they take an enormous amount of abuse. They are the second-most-often remodeled room in the house. Materials used in the bathroom should be durable and attractive.

1 Lighting. It is very important to have enough good light so that there are no shadows in the mirror area. This requires at least one light near the center of the ceiling and additional lighting over the counter area. Strip lighting (light bar) should run the entire length of the counter. Night lights are useful, particularly in households with young children.

2 Flooring. For practicality, durability, and attractiveness, ceramic tile is the product of choice. And, of course, it is impervious to water. The choice of pattern and color is limitless, and grout is available in a variety of complementary colors as well. Set on the diagonal, ceramic tiles can be quite striking.

BEFORE

AFTER

Moving the toilet in this hallway bathroom created greater privacy as well as a more attractive hallway view (see floor plan on page 75).

A dressing table, whirlpool tub, tile flooring, brass fixtures, and good lighting are all elements of an attractive bathroom. Strip lighting in this bathroom is elegantly hidden behind wooden valances (see page 96 for directions).

3   Toilet location. Toilets are not particularly thought of as glamorous, and I prefer not to view one when I open a bathroom door. Privacy is an issue, too — if the door is inadvertently opened when the toilet is in use, how much nicer to have a limited view! Compartmentalizing the toilet usually requires one additional wall to separate it from the other fixtures — not a huge investment for the benefits gained.

4   Separate shower stall. Separate shower stalls, whether one-piece-molded or tile, are easier to get into and easier to clean, and therefore more efficient for day-to-day use, than tub-shower combinations.

5   Water control valve. A water control valve is a mechanism that ensures the consistency of the water temperature. When you step into the shower and turn on the faucet at your preferred setting, you will get the same predetermined mix of hot and cold water every time. No more fumbling around when you're half asleep, trying to get the water temperature adjusted just right. This valve can be installed on most faucets.

6   Whirlpool tub. For a while during the 1980s, the trend was to install a large hot tub inside the home. But there were drawbacks — moisture problems, the size of the appliance, the nuisance of maintaining the correct chemical balance, and the weight of the tub when filled with water. But the luxury of jets of water pulsating on tired muscles was still something many people wanted. Hence the popularity of the whirlpool tub, a miniversion of the hot tub. If it is the size of a standard bathtub, no additional structural support is required. Whirlpool sizes vary, but they can be had in conventional tub sizes.

7   Dressing table. How can you put on your pierced earrings without using both hands and sitting up close to a mirror? Blow-drying your hair with a brush takes two hands and is much easier if you're sitting in front of a dressing table on which to set down a brush or curling iron. Makeup, too, is easier to apply if you're sitting down. A well-lit dressing table is convenient in the bathroom, particularly next to the sink. A chair or stool the right height completes the package.

8   Brass fixtures. Brass emits a very elegant glow. Incorporate it in stylish faucets for the tub, sinks, and shower, towel bars, and even a lever for the toilet, and the bathroom is ablaze in its rays. Brass fixtures are dressy and worth the price difference over chrome.

9   Heat and light fixture. "One-stop shopping" could describe some of the best bathroom ceiling fixtures. Nu-tome and other manufacturers offer a heat/light/vent/nightlight all combined in one unit. An electric ceiling heater produces more warmth than infrared lights and is sized according to the square footage of the bathroom. I recommend fans (directly vented to the outside) even if there is an operable window.

10 Storage space. You need a closet to hold towels, bedroom linens, toiletries, and a clothes hamper. It doesn't need to be deep. In fact, 12″ is perfect; nothing gets shoved to the back. You can install a floor-to-ceiling closet that is 6′ wide, enclose it with folding doors, and arrange the shelving to fit your needs.

Top 10 Kid's Bedroom Features

Having their own room that reflects their own interests is important to children, especially when they hit the teenage years. Even if you have a couple children sharing a bedroom, certain built-in features can identify each child's own special space and help define each one's own living area.

1   Desk with shelves. A desk with bookshelves mounted above it is very useful.

2   Closets with organizer shelves and hamper. Even if you can't make you chilren clean their room regularly, having well-organized places to store things will provide some incentive.

3   Dresser.

4   Wall lamp.

5   Shelves for toys and personal objects. Often collections of favorite items or hobby equipment makes a pleasing decorating accent.

6   Full-length mirror. Mounted on inside of closet door.

7   Bulletin board.

8   Nightstand with lamp.

9   Attractively framed art or photos on wall. A collection of fun photos from camp, vacation, or a school trip adds to the personal quality of the room.

10 Comfortable chair.

DISPLAYING A CHILD'S TREASURES

A dramatic focal point can be created by using a child's treasures as a decorative accent around the bed. Try mounting shelves along the wall over a bed or desk to display a collection of porcelain angels, for instance, sports trophies, teddy bears or other stuffed animals, photos of friends or family, or ceramic pieces made in art class. Another way to create a focal point is to hang a large handmade fabric hanging, a collection of original artwork, or school pennants on the walls.

Top 10 Laundry Room Features

With a tile-lined drip-dry closet in the laundry room, makeshift clotheslines are unnecessary.

A separate laundry room is the ultimate in efficient housekeeping. Any clothes that have not yet been washed, sorted, or ironed are at least out of sight.

1 **Sink and counter.** A large sink next to the washer and dryer comes in handy not only for laundry purposes but for potting plants, cleaning paintbrushes, and washing a small dog. And how can you go wrong with extra counter space, particularly for hobbies and crafts?

2 **Drip-dry closet.** An open closet lined with ceramic tile makes a great place for hanging damp clothes to air-dry. A drain is not necessary since clothes that have been spun in the washer will air-dry without dripping. At long last — no more pantyhose hanging on the shower rod.

3 **Built-in ironing board.** Allow space for an iron and an outlet.

4 **Telephone.**

5 **Space for an extra refrigerator and/or freezer.**

6 **Sewing or craft area.**

7 **Built-in cupboards.** These are great for storing cleaning and laundry supplies.

8 **Attractive and coordinated colors.** When decorating a laundry room, choose colors that are pleasing and easy to live with. Given the nature of a laundry room, there will often be piles of things around, so a soothing background color scheme helps.

9 **Waterproof floor.**

10 **Excellent lighting.**

Finding, Creating, and Transforming Space

One of the greatest home decorating challenges is designing space that accommodates the various needs of all the people living in your home. As these needs change, you can often rearrange the furnishings in a particular room to meet new needs. For instance, if the need arises for a family computer, you may be able to make room in a closet to hold a roll-out computer desk. However, there are other desires that simply require more space — no way around it. There are several ways I've reconfigured or transformed existing space in houses to create new rooms.

Expanding a Kitchen

The kitchen is the most important and heavily used room in the house. Make it an enjoyable, efficient, and attractive room and you will increase your home's resale potential as well.

What should you do if your kitchen is too small to be efficient and you love the rest of the house? You can push the walls back in some direction, depending on the floor layout and how much space you can spare from other rooms.

Taking Space from a Bedroom to Enlarge the Kitchen

Problem: The only way I can expand my kitchen is to take space from a bedroom. Is this wise? How can I do this without making my bedroom seem cramped?

Solution: If taking space from an adjoining bedroom will allow you to create a more functional cooking and/or eating area, then do it. You can modify the bedroom to meet your needs by creating built-ins, which take less space. Build in a dresser unit around the bed, or build in the bed and a drawer unit next to it. (One note, though, when considering resale potential: Most people want a large master bedroom, so avoid taking space from the master if possible.)

Kitchen expansion plan: Taking space from the closet in the adjoining bedroom creates room to recess the stove and refrigerator, build counter and cabinets around them, and then add a cooking island in the middle of the room.

DESIGN POSSIBILITIES

Here are several examples of adjoining spaces that could potentially be used to expand the kitchen. After reading these descriptions, take a careful look at the areas around your kitchen and see if you can apply some of the ideas.

Example 1. Say your kitchen is adjacent to a bathroom with a poorly tiled bathtub running parallel to the kitchen wall. In the bathroom is a closet that could be removed and replaced with a shower stall. The solution then is to remove the tub, install a new shower stall (which will be more efficient than the deteriorating tub unit), and expand the kitchen into the 5′x30″ space left by the bathtub.

The result is a kitchen that looks twice as big and presents new possibilities for arranging the appliances and furnishings efficiently. The stove that had been sitting out in the middle of the floor can now be recessed into the former bathtub area, with additional counter space created next to it.

Example 2. Say your kitchen runs parallel to an 11′x2′ bedroom closet. You could take 8′ of the closet (leaving a 3′ closet for the bedroom) to create a niche for the refrigerator, built-in microwave, and built-in double oven, units that now sit out in the room. Recessing these appliances creates a generous-sized central kitchen area that can accommodate an island with a cooktop. If you have an older refrigerator, install a good-sized vent at the bottom of the wall behind it for air circulation (as illustrated below).

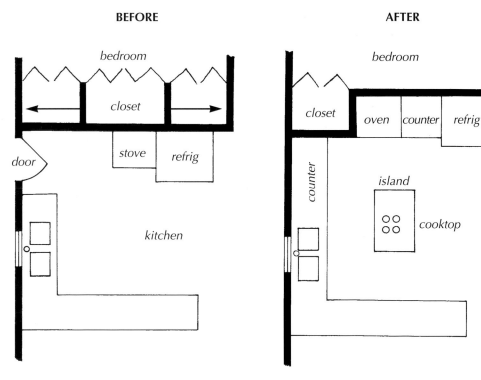

BEFORE

AFTER

Transforming a Basement

One of the most common "opportunities" homeowners have for creating more living space is a poured-concrete basement. Walk-out basements (where a portion of the basement opens to the outside via a window or door) are especially common in ranch-style houses that were built in the 1950s.

Basement foundation garages provide a marvelous opportunity for creating additional living space. The garage door can be replaced with a picture window to bring in needed light and then the space can be transformed to be much more than a "basement." In fact, some builders call the result a "dual-level" home.

SUGGESTED RENOVATIONS

There are several key steps in transforming a basement into dual-level living quarters. Most of these require hiring professionals, unless you have building expertise. However, these suggestions will help you decide what kind of work you want done.

Create more light. The aim in creating dual-level living space is to bring light into as large an area of the basement as possible. One way to begin to do this is to treat the stairway leading to the basement like a grand staircase. First, remove the door at the top of the stairs and structurally increase the size of the door opening leading to the lower level. Expand the width of the stairway to

Cutting a window well in the foundation is key to opening up a dark basement area and making it into a light, livable room.

A Note of Caution on Basement Construction

Before you begin construction in your basement, be sure to check carefully for water leakage. If there is a crack in the foundation through which moisture seeps in, this must be corrected before you can begin construction. To do this, the outside area surrounding the cracked foundation should be excavated to the footings and some method of waterproofing applied. Seek professional advice about damp-proofing or water-proofing before you invest any money in renovations.

This gracious stairway was created from a narrow enclosed basement stairway, bringing light and a spacious feeling to the lower level.

close to 4′ if possible. To do this, the structure around the stairway must be reheaded (parts cut away and the remainder reinforced). A skilled carpenter should have no problem making this structural change. Even if you are planning to do most of the basement renovation yourself, unless you are experienced at carpentry, don't take this one on alone.

To gain additional light and create a room at the far end of the basement, install a window well. This excavation work really is worth it — it will make the room feel like an above-grade room and will bring it up to code for fire and ventilation. The window should be sized according to the square footage of the room. Check your state building codes before laying out your plans. The Massachusetts Building Code requires that natural light be provided by a window of not less than 8 percent of the floor area. I recommend consulting a civil engineer or someone skilled in this field before you begin construction.

Installing a window well. This requires excavating an area next to the foundation. The depth is determined by the building code in the area where you live; in the East it is necessary to put our frost walls 4′ below the frost line. You will need to hire a company that specializes in cutting concrete to cut a window in the foundation, but the cost is worth it. If you try to do it yourself with inadequate equipment, it could literally take you days. After the window hole is cut, footings are poured and the walls for the well are formed and poured. Pipe is then laid for drainage, stones layered on top of the pipe, and the area is backfilled. The drainage pipe must go "to light," meaning that it should slope downward until it comes out of the ground on your own property or into a dry well. A dry well is a large hole (approximately 5′x5′) filled with stone.

You will need to insulate the concrete walls of your new room. To do this, stud the walls out with 2″x4″x16″ o.c. (o.c. means that the studs are spaced 16″ apart); 2″x4″x8′ pine studs are used by carpenters to frame out walls. Run wiring and plumbing pipes, then put in batts of fiberglass insulation and install Sheetrock. Allow an airspace of 1″ between the studs and the cement walls. Do not use plastic as a vapor barrier because it could prevent the house from breathing. (You do not want any condensation that might seep through foundation walls to be trapped there by a plastic barrier.)

Installing flooring. I recommend laying wood floors in the basement area. To do this, you begin by placing heavy, 6-ml plastic sheeting over the entire basement floor as a vapor barrier. Flooring sleepers, or supports, can be made of 1″x2″ pressure-treated lumber (p.t.), 16″ o.c., and attached to the cement floor with concrete nails. Keep the size of the sleepers to a minimum to maximize headroom. (P.T. lumber is used any time extra protection is necessary because of proximity to dampness or water.) Place 1″ rigid insulation between the sleepers and cover the entire area with tarpaper. Screw wide pine boards to the sleepers (if there is not enough space to use nails). Sleepers may be 1″ or less, which does not offer enough girth to hold a nail. (For information on finishing wood floors, see pages 117 to 119.)

CREATING A BASEMENT FLOOR PLAN

What is the best way to use the new space created by redoing the basement? The options are numerous. One important thing to keep in mind is that you want to make the most of the light coming in from the entrance to the basement (where the garage door was originally located). Keeping large open corridors between the rooms will allow the light to reach the largest possible area.

Following is a sample plan I created for a basement that originally had a fireplace and a half-bath but no other partitions. Once I finished the work on the walls, flooring, windows, and staircase as described in the previous section, I divided the area into the following spaces:

- Full-sized bathroom with shower
- Room approximately 11′x14′ with a 6′ closet
- Walk-in cedar closet
- Laundry room
- Family room with fireplace opening to a sitting area
- Mudroom connecting to the garage
- Utility room for the furnace
- Storage room with workbench

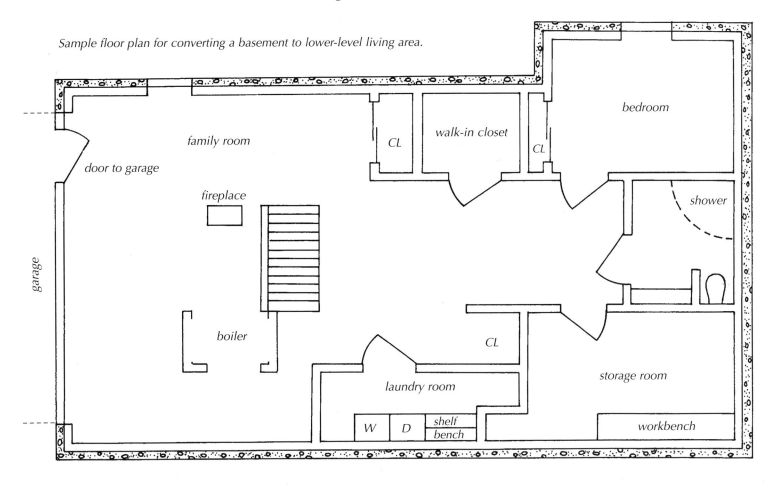

Sample floor plan for converting a basement to lower-level living area.

Expanding Other Rooms and Spaces

Each house presents its own particular challenges when it comes to creating additional space. Here are a few examples that may apply to your home.

BATHROOM

If you have a bathroom that's too small, weigh the pros and cons of taking space from an adjoining room. For example, say your bathroom adjoins a small bedroom with a sloping ceiling. Although the bedroom is small to begin with, taking 3′ from it won't affect the actual living space much because of the sloped ceiling. If this is the only bathroom in the house, the benefits of a larger bathroom outweigh the loss of space in the bedroom.

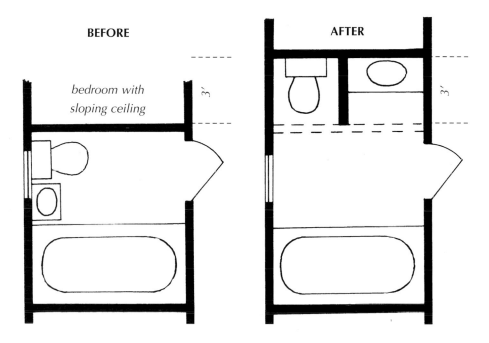

BEFORE   **AFTER**

bedroom with sloping ceiling

3′   3′

Bathroom expansion plan: *Taking 3′ of space from an adjoining bedroom allows for a more comfortable and spacious toilet and sink arrangement.*

CLOSETS

Example 1. If you live in an old house, you may be familiar with the dilemma of a shallow closet with the door offset to one side, making it impossible to reach the clothes hanging deep inside at the opposite end of the closet. The solution is to open up the other end of the closet by cutting an opening for an additional closet door.

BEFORE

window

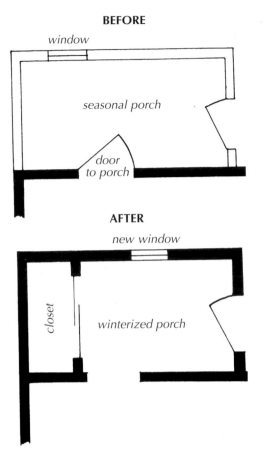

seasonal porch

*door
to porch*

AFTER

new window

winterized porch

closet

Example 2: *Plan for creating a closet in a winterized entryway from a back porch.*

If possible, find a door in another area of the house that matches your closet door. This could be a door that is seldom used (like between a kitchen and dining area). It is more important that the two closet doors match, even if it's necessary to put a new door in the spot where you remove the old one. Cut an opening next to the closet door and build a door casing to fit the matching door. The final result will be a two-door, very accessible 6' closet.

Example 2. You have a seasonal back porch that could become a new, winterized entryway with a 6' coat closet, but there is a window in the way of the proposed closet.

Remove the interior porch door permanently, take off the existing Sheetrock, frame in the window approximately 2' over, out of the way of the proposed closet, install new wiring, insulate the walls and ceiling, and frame in the new 6'x20" closet.

Example 3. Imagine you live in a small A-frame house that seems to have no room for a washer and dryer or a coat closet. The open 12'x12' hall is large enough to accommodate a good-sized closet. By building a 2x4 framed wall from floor to ceiling between the kitchen door and the left side of the kitchen wall and enclosing it with bifold doors that open from either side, you have a neat-looking laundry closet. An adjoining coat closet could be added.

BEFORE

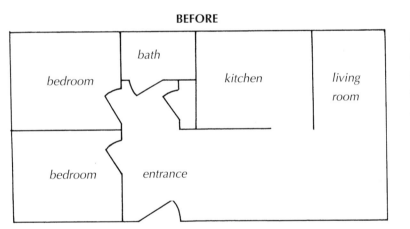

bath

bedroom

kitchen

*living
room*

bedroom

entrance

Example 3:

Plan for creating a washer/dryer closet from space in the front hall.

AFTER

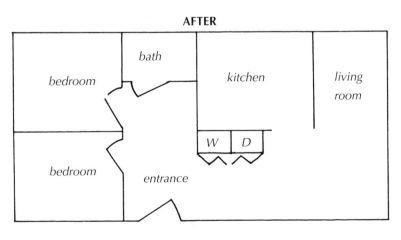

bath

bedroom

kitchen

*living
room*

W *D*

bedroom

entrance

Example 4. Many people who own older houses are faced with the problem of square bedrooms that do not have closets. Bedrooms need closets, but closets that simply project out into a room look like an afterthought rather than an integral part of the overall design. You can avoid this problem by combining the closet with other adjoining structural features such as the bed (option 1), or actually building the closet in with an extended set of shelves or a built-in desk with shelves over it (option 2).

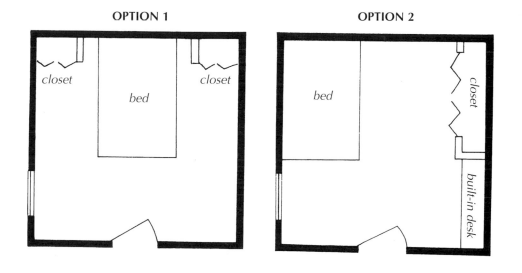

Option 2, front view of closet and desk.

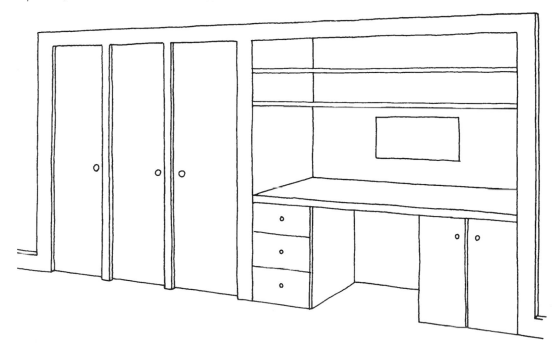

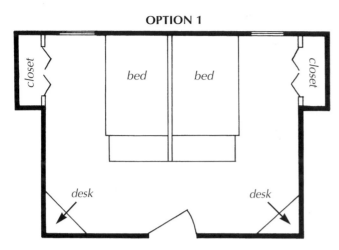

OPTION 1

closet | bed | bed | closet
desk | | | desk

OPTION 2

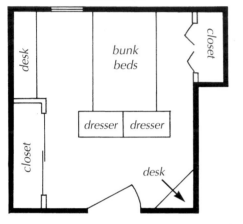

desk | bunk beds | closet
closet | dresser | dresser
| | desk

Children's bedroom space: *Two options for creating separate spaces for children sharing a room and making the most of the existing space.*

BEDROOM SPACE

How to create privacy for children sharing a bedroom is another common dilemma. Consider the case of an 11'x14' room. This size lends itself beautifully to the construction of a semipermanent divider wall that is attached to the two bed frames, (option 1 as illustrated). This particular arrangement works well because the door is centered and there is closet space on each side of the room. A possible variation for a smaller room is to build bunk beds into a center unit (see option 2). Push the bed unit closer to the side with an existing closet and build in a closet/desk unit for the other side, keeping the window arrangement in mind.

If this idea is appealing to your teenage kids, suggest they work to save for a carpenter or building materials.

WINDOWS AND VISUAL SPACE

A bay window can add actual square footage as well as visually enlarge a room if it is constructed full length. There are two ways to add a bay window.

Method 1: A hole is cut in the wall for an 8'-wide bay window 2' off the floor. The window unit is 5' high and comes in one piece. This type of bay window protrudes from the face of the house, creating a shelf or very deep window sill. It is designed to have a shelf like a window seat.

Method 2: This bay window is 7' high and requires foundational support. A floor must be constructed in the bay projection at the same level as the existing floor in the room. This particular design projects 3' from the original wall, thus increasing the room area by approximately 20 square feet. Because of the foundation work, it is expensive to construct.

Windows can also be used very effectively to expand a space visually. Changing a small room with one existing window to include a window wall is amazingly effective. A window wall is a 6' patio door or wider window unit. Often an improvement of this kind increases the livability of a house an inestimable amount.

Another way to visually enlarge a space is to eliminate a wall and doorway to the basement. You'll usually gain the width of the stairway, which can be closed off at the bottom of the stairs. If you have interior doors that serve no good purpose, remove them, too.

Is it worthwhile to spend money to open up a room visually even though you won't gain floor space? Yes, yes, yes!

Basic Sewing Techniques for Home Decorating

There are two major motivations for sewing home decorating projects yourself: getting exactly the right look and saving money. Getting the right look means finding the right color or pattern fabric that will pull the room or house together.

As discussed in Chapter 1 in the section "Select a Color Scheme," color is the most important factor in decorating. Think of how you accessorize a basic black dress, perhaps with a particular scarf that brings out the color of your eyes or blends with the color of your jacket. If you add earrings with a dash of the scarf color, the effect is further enhanced. The same is true for your house. The right color combinations and accessories will do more to tie your decor together than any other element of your home decorating.

Sometimes the only way to get the right fabric for your home is to pick it out yourself. Having to rely on finding the right ready-made drapes and curtains is limiting. Being able to sew expands your decorating options by opening up nearly limitless fabric options.

The first step in making your own window treatments is deciding on a style. I've included instructions here for four styles of window treatments: drapes, curtains, swags, and valances, with many variations on each style. You may be surprised by how easy it is to make your own, and by how much money you can save in the process.

Drapes

If the style you are trying to achieve is formal or you have a large south-facing picture window, you are probably going to want floor-length drapes. While working with that much fabric, and trying to achieve all those pleats, may seem like a formidable task, it's actually quite easy with a few simple techniques.

PLEATER-TAPE DRAPES

One of the easiest ways to make drapes is with pleater tape, a fabric tape that you sew onto your curtain fabric. The tape contains pockets for hooks that automatically create pleats once the hooks are inserted into the pockets. Pleater-tape drapes are easy to launder; all you have to do is remove the hooks. If any pressing is necessary, it's easy, too, because without the hooks in it the fabric is flat.

Once you've set up a small sewing area, you're on the way to making your own customized window treatments.

DETERMINING FABRIC AMOUNT

You can adjust the number of pleats in a pleater-tape drape by changing the number of hooks you insert: the more hooks, the more fabric width taken up in pleats. This gives you some flexibility in the amount of fabric you need to allow for each panel. For a standard-sized window, use a full width of fabric for each side (*not* a pair), and then add hooks as needed to hang. Ideally, the hooks should be equally spaced. But you can fudge a bit on either end of the drape by making a single pleat or a triple pleat — whatever works to take up the remaining fabric.

You should allow an extra 2″ to 3″ in the finished width of each drape to allow the traverse rod to move with ease into the closed position, with the drapes just overlapping.

PROBLEM SOLVER

How Much Fabric to Buy

Problem: How do you know how much fabric to buy to make floor-length drapes for a 36″-wide window?

Solution: Begin by measuring the length from the floor to the spot where the hook will hang in the traverse rod hole and add 2″ to allow for the rod width. Say this length is 7′. Add 7″ for the top hem and 4″ for the bottom hem for a total of 11″, which can be rounded off to 12″ or 1′ (since fabric is purchased in yards, not inches). Add this to the 7′ for a total of 8′, which is 2⅔ yards. With one panel on each side of the window, the total yardage necessary is 5⅓ yards.

To calculate the total cost of fabric for a room with four standard windows, multiply the yardage per window by 4. The total count for the room is 21⅓ plus a little extra. Round this off to 23 yards. It is always an insurance policy to have a little extra in case you measure incorrectly and need to recut a piece or wish to use extra for covering a stool, etc. Knowing you need 23 yards, multiply the amount of fabric times the cost per yard.

What is the look you want, and what is your budget? Before you buy, check around to see what else is available in your budget range. Remember to include in the cost the price of lining fabric, pleater tape and hooks (if you use them), traverse rods (if you don't already have them), and thread.

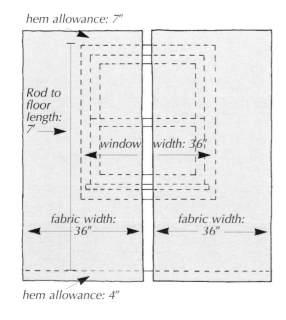

hem allowance: 7″

Rod to floor length: 7′

window width: 36″

fabric width: 36″   fabric width: 36″

hem allowance: 4″

To calculate the amount of fabric needed for floor-length drapes, measure the distance from the rod to the floor, add 2″ for the rod width, then add 7″ at the top and 4″ at the bottom for hems. Finally, double this total to cover both sides of the window.

Instructions for Pleater-Tape Drapes

These directions are for a standard-sized window, approximately 3' wide. For a wider window, use the same basic technique but start with a wider width of fabric, obtained by sewing two or more widths together (see tip #6 on page 84).

1. Cut fabric for each drape (as instructed on page 84).
2. Finish the side edges of each drape by turning each edge under 1", then folding it again, as shown. Make sure that the unprinted edge of the fabric (selvage) is taken in by this fold. Stitch along the edge, using a thread color that is the same color as the fabric or the background color of the fabric.
3. The pleater tape is about 4" wide. To accommodate that width, fold the top edge of the drape down 6" on the wrong side of the fabric. Turn the raw edge under 1" to make a finished hem. Press, and stitch next to the fold. (The pleater tape is placed ½" down from the folded top edge, accounting for the extra 1".)
4. Pin the pleater tape across the entire width of the top of each drape ½" from the top of the fabric (on the wrong side of the fabric). Be sure the "top" arrow on the tape is pointing up and the pocket side of the tape is facing out. Stitch ¼" from the top of the tape; then stitch ¼" from the bottom, being careful not to stitch across the pockets.
5. Insert a hook (to form a pleat) at each end of the drape and one in the middle; add additional hooks to get the desired width and fullness. Adjustments can be made when you see how the drape hangs. If the prongs on each hook take up too much fabric, use only two. Two-pronged hooks use less fabric than three-pronged ones. Each pleat should have the same number of folds. It may take a little experimenting to work out the first drape — then repeat the procedure for the rest.
6. Hang the drape on the traverse rod and mark or pin up the hem. Remove the drape from the rod, press the fabric at the hemline, and hem by machine. Weights (small metal squares) can be sewn into the inside hem corners to weigh down the edges if desired. (These can be purchased at a fabric store.)

Pleats are easy to make with pleater tape and multi-pronged hooks.

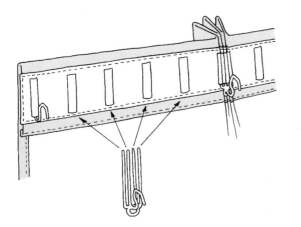

Drapes Without Pleater Tape

To make drapes without using pleater tape, you need a sewing machine that is capable of sewing through several layers of fabric to make pleats. Many lightweight portable machines are not that powerful.

DETERMINING FABRIC AMOUNT

The basic method is to use one width of fabric for each side of the drape, and then figure out the number of pleats you can allow given the width of your window. If your fabric is 54″ wide, allow 2″ on each side for hemming (4″ total), which leaves you with 50″.

If one panel must cover half a 36″ window, allow about 20″ of fabric (18″ width plus 2″ thrown in for good measure) just to cover half the window width. This leaves 30″ of fabric for pleats. If the pleat allowance is 4″ per pleat, you can have seven pleats with a little slack left over. The pleats should be about 2¾″ apart. Put a pleat at each end about ½″ from the edge of the drape.

Instructions for Drapes Without Pleater Tape
1. Pin 4″ pleats together on right side of fabric, allowing about 2¾″ between pleats.
2. On right side of fabric, stitch a straight seam along each pleat line to about 4″ from the top of the drape.
3. On the front of the drape, make two folds in each pleat to form three smaller pleats. Stitch these smaller pleats together by hand with a repeated overhand stitch placed about 3″ from the top of the drape.

On the front of the drape, fold each pleat into three smaller pleats and stitch together by hand.

Pleats are spaced about 2¾″ apart.

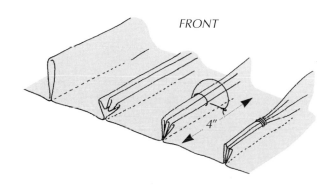

BACK

2¾″

2″

FRONT

4″

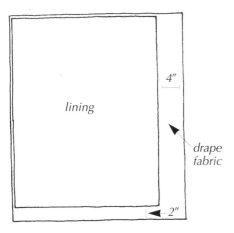

Cut the lining fabric narrower and shorter than your drape fabric (above). The finished edges of the drape will fold over to the back on both sides (below).

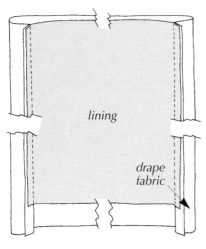

This lined drape is then turned inside out and pressed.

Instructions for Lining Drapes

Lining drapes is not difficult — just an extra step. This should be done once you have your panels cut (or pieced) to the desired width and length.

1. Measure the length and width of the drape. Cut a piece of lining fabric that measures 4″ narrower and 2″ shorter than the drape piece.

2. Place the drape and lining pieces together (right side to right side) and pin together, with the top and side edges even (the lining will be 2″ short at the bottom). Stitch a ¾″-seam along the two long sides.

3. Press the seams open, turn the lined drape inside out and press the finished edges, allowing the drapery fabric to turn under 2″ on each side. Baste-stitch the fabric and lining together ½″ from the top edge so the fabric won't slip when you start sewing on the pleater tape.

4. Once you have completed the top of the drapes (with the technique you desire), hem the lining separately from the drapery fabric.

TIPS FOR PERFECT FABRIC MEASURING, CUTTING, AND PIECING

To ensure that your finished window treatments will be the precise length you want, I recommend taking the following steps before you begin sewing.

1. Install the curtain rod so you will know exactly where the drapery hook or fabric will be positioned on the rod.

2. Determine the length of the drape (if it's to float on the floor, add inches).

3. If making window treatments that will be laundered, prewash the fabric.

4. It is better to use a less expensive fabric that you can buy plenty of (including extra to match patterns) than to skimp on a more expensive fabric.

5. Rule of thumb for the window width when making drapes: Have a final width of fabric that is at least two but not more than three times the window width.

6. To create a drape or curtain from two or more widths of fabric, you will need to join the long panels. Several guidelines will help you avoid the most obvious pitfalls. First, always place the two lengths of fabric right side to right side (thus sewing on the wrong side). Second, before you cut the lengths of fabric, be sure to match any repeating pattern. Check carefully for any recurring pattern that is easy to identify. Measure the needed length of fabric from this point and cut. Then find the place where the same pattern occurs again, cut off any excess fabric above it, and measure and cut a matching length. Dealing with wide pieces of fabric is not hard but it is a bit cumbersome when the material is heavy or lined.

7. Use a carpenter's aluminum 4′ T square as a guide for marking fabric before you cut. Line up the selvage edge of the fabric with the table edge, place the T square against the same edge, and mark a perpendicular line across the fabric.

Curtains

There are many style possibilities for curtains, including tab curtains, gathered cafés, and a variety of swags. Most of these are easy to make. There are even curtains you can make without sewing.

NO-SEW SWAG CURTAINS

Swag curtains don't require sewing, although, if you want them to last for several years, it would be wise to hem the edges by either gluing or sewing them. It is important not to skimp on the fabric; an average-sized window can take approximately 7 to 8 yards. Even with this requirement, swags can be very reasonable if you buy inexpensive fabric at a discount store (even unbleached fabric or lining material will work) or bed sheets on sale. Or use a set of discarded drapes. Swags can be made in three different lengths:

This simple swag is made from one continuous length of fabric looped over metal hooks.

- Valance (requires 2 to 3 yards of fabric per window)
- Casement, falling just to the bottom of the window casing (requires 5 to 6 yards of fabric per window)
- Floor-length (requires 7 to 8 yards of fabric per window)

Tacked Swags. This style of no-sew swags doesn't even require curtain rods, because it entails tacking the fabric directly to the window casement. You can even leave the edges raw or, if you prefer, finish them by hemming with a machine or turning up and attaching with fabric glue.

Instructions for Tacked No-Sew Swags
To make no-sew swags you will need:
- Thumb tacks
- Small hammer
- Scissors
- Fabric glue
- Tape measure

1. Before cutting your final length of fabric, do a "trial run" to figure out exactly how long a piece of fabric you want to use. To do this, follow the instructions for step 2 (on next page) with your full length of fabric, pushing the thumbtacks in just far enough to hold the fabric for a few minutes. Adjust the swag until you are satisfied with the look and mark the finished length you desire. Then take the fabric down and cut.

2. Mark the center of the length of fabric and hammer a thumbtack through the fabric into the upper center edge of the window casement (where it won't be visible head-on). Then tack the fabric at both corners of the upper edge of the casement; if the fabric is very heavy, use more tacks to hold the weight.

3. Cut two strips of fabric, each 1½" wide by 30" long. Finish the edges if you desire, or just press them under. If these curtains are intended to be fairly temporary, raw edges will suffice. I have used this method with a patterned fabric, where the raw edges weren't noticeable. However, if you know you'll be laundering the fabric, you should create finished strips by folding each strip in half (right sides together), stitching a seam along the edge, and then turning the strip right side out.

4. Place one strip under the swag fabric hanging on the upper left side of the window and thumbtack it to the casing, leaving a tail of about 10" (see illustration). Do the same with the other fabric strip on the right side of the window.

5. Bring the loose end of each fabric strip up and around the swag fabric; join it with the end attached to the casing, either by tying a bow or thumbtacking it.

6. Adjust the fabric swags so that they fall evenly on both sides and the side selvage edges are turned under.

7. If the curtains are too long, you can adjust the length simply by cutting off any extra fabric or adjusting the drape of the swag to be fuller. If you're making matching swags for other windows of the same size, take this first one down and use it as a pattern for cutting the others. Using this technique, you can make curtains for a whole house in just a couple of hours.

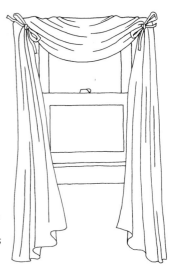

A no-sew swag is attached to the upper edge of the window casement with thumb tacks (left) and then tied at the two upper corners (right).

Looped Swags. This is another style of no-sew swags that is easy to make from a straight length of fabric. To hang looped swags, I recommended using wooden holders and dowels. Inexpensive unfinished holders can be purchased wherever curtain rods are sold. These are mounted onto the window casing with screws. For the rod, look for a wooden dowel or closet rod at a lumber store; they are available in just about any length you desire. Finish the rod by painting or staining it, or covering it in the same fabric as the curtain — a very effective and inexpensive way to make the rod attractive.

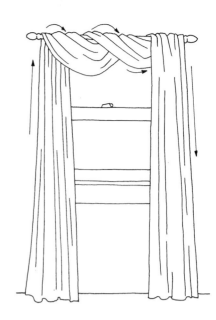

A looped swag simply involves wrapping fabric around a dowel road — an elegant look with just a little effort.

Instructions for Looped Swags

1. Mount the wooden rod and holder on the window casing, as instructed above.
2. Drape your fabric over the left side of the rod, adjusting it to the length you wish it to hang.
3. Loop the other end once around the rod; using straight pins, pin from the back side several places to secure the left-side panel. Be sure to turn the side edges of the fabric under as you work so that the selvage is not showing on either side.
4. Make additional loose loops of fabric around the rod to achieve the look you like; pin wherever necessary to maintain even folds.
5. When you make the last loop on the right side of the rod, match the length of fabric draping down that side to be even with the left side; cut off any excess fabric, if necessary. Pin the right-side panel in place.
6. To finish the raw edges of the fabric, turn to the wrong side of the fabric and secure with fabric glue.

Swags can be created in three lengths: valance, casement, and floor-length.

valance swag

casement swag

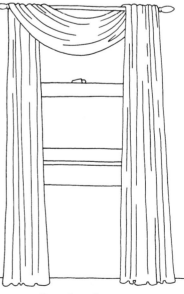

floor-length swag

CAFÉ CURTAINS

Café curtains are a simple design that offers a great deal of flexibility. They can be used on the lower part of a double hung window, on both parts, or with a valance. You can make a valance using the same design, just much shorter.

Café curtains can be hung on standard 1"-wide rods, or, as I prefer, 3"-wide rods. The wider width looks more substantial.

Determining width of fabric needed. This style of curtain uses just one wide piece of fabric for each window. To figure out how wide this piece needs to be, measure the width of your window and double that measurement. For instance, if the window is 36" wide, you'll need a 72"-wide piece of fabric. You'll probably have to sew two lengths of fabric together to get this width. (Don't forget to match the pattern if necessary, as described on page 84.)

Determining length of fabric needed. Measure the width of your curtain rod; double this amount and add 1" to allow a bit of leeway in your sewing. If, for example, your rod is 1½" wide, double that plus 1" is 4". Then add ½" for the hem allowance and 1" for a "ruffled" fabric edge above the rod, for a total of 5½" for the top of the curtain.

Now, measure from the top of the installed rod to the point where you want the bottom edge of your curtain. Add to this number 2½" for the bottom hem. Finally, add in the 5½" allowance for the top of the curtain and you have the total length of the fabric you need to cut for each window.

Instructions for Café Curtains

I suggest trying the steps 2, 3, and 4 on a 10" by 12" scrap piece of fabric to check the accuracy of the measurements and make sure the pocket fits on your rod before making the actual curtain.

1. To hem the sides of your curtain, press under ½" along each side (turning the raw edge under if you want a finished edge) and stitch close to the edge.
2. Fold under ½" of the raw edge at the top of the curtain and press. Then fold under the top 5" of fabric to form the upper hem, which will be the pocket for the rod. Press and stitch along the bottom edge of this pocket.
3. Stitch a straight seam ½" from the top of the pocket, creating a strip of fabric above the rod that looks a little like a ruffle. (You can add a ruffle to the bottom edge of the curtain, too, if desired.)
4. Slip the curtain on the rod and hang on the brackets.
5. Pin up the hem at the desired length and remove from the rod. Press along hemline. Turn the raw edge under ½" and press. Stitch close to the edge.

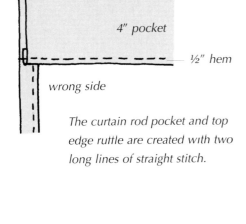

1" ruffle

4" pocket

½" hem

wrong side

The curtain rod pocket and top edge ruffle are created with two long lines of straight stitch.

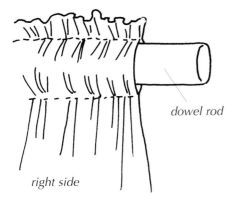

dowel rod

right side

The finished café curtain is gathered as it's put on the dowel rod.

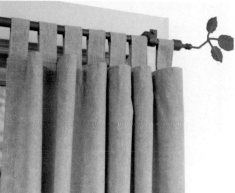

Tab curtains are great for a casual country look and are relatively easy to make.

TAB CURTAINS

If you prefer a country look, tab curtains may be just right for many of your rooms. They are relatively simple to make and require a minimum amount of fabric because too much fullness is not desirable. The only sewing involved in making these curtains is turning under hems on the side, top, and bottom, and attaching the tab loops. This last step is the tricky part. It involves making loops from the same fabric as the curtain and sewing them, evenly spaced, onto the curtain.

Tab curtains are seldom lined, and they ordinarily fit within the windowsill, which makes them a fine choice for showing off detailed window casings. Tabs can also be made floor length for patio doors. Hang tab curtains on curtain rods made from wooden dowels (see page 99 for instructions), which add an authentic design element and show off the tabs to best advantage.

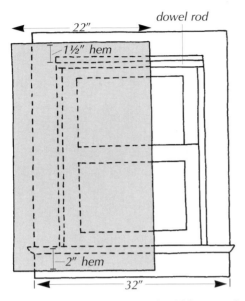

Determining width and length of fabric needed for tab curtain panel.

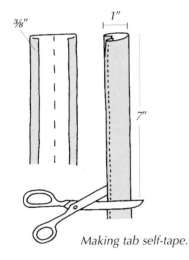

Making tab self-tape.

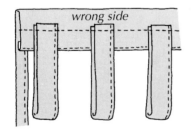

Stitch the evenly spaced tabs to the curtain panel with the loops pointing down on the wrong side.

Determining fabric amount. To make window-length curtains for a standard-sized window, you'll need approximately 5 yards of fabric, with 1 of those yards allocated for tabs. You can make 48 tabs from 1 yard, which will easily be enough for three pairs of two-panel curtains. You usually use about 8 tabs per side of curtain, but this can vary.

Determining width. The curtain panel should be only slightly wider than the area to be covered. For example, if the inside width of the window is 32″, divide 32″ in half for two panels — each panel will be 16″. To this measurement, add 4″ for a little fullness and 1″ on each side to allow for hemming, for a total of 22″.

Determining length. As with all window treatments, the most accurate method of measuring for length is to install the curtain rods first. Measure from ½″ below the rod to the bottom of the inside frame of the window. To this measurement add 1½″ for the top hem and 2″ for the bottom hem.

Instructions for Tab Curtains

1. To hem the sides of each curtain panel, fold ½″ of fabric along each side to the wrong side and press. Fold over ½″ again (to enclose raw edge) and press. Stitch ¼″ from the edge.

2. To make hem at top of panel, fold ½″ of fabric to wrong side and press. Then fold that edge down 1″ and press. Stitch along the edge. Do *not* hem the bottom of the panel until after step 10, when the tabs are sewn on.

3. To make the tab self-tape, cut strips of fabric measuring 3½″ wide and 1 yard long. Be very accurate with these measurements. One yard of 36″ fabric will produce approximately forty 7″ tab strips. You will need about 16 tabs for each window.

4. Press the long raw edges of each strip inside ⅜″. Then, fold each strip in half lengthwise, wrong sides together, and pin the folded edges together evenly to make strips approximately 1″ wide. Stitch a ⅜″ seam along the length of each strip.

5. Cut each long strip into 7″ tab strips. If you have a dowel that is greater than 1″ in diameter, cut a 7″ test strip of scrap fabric first to make sure that it fits comfortably around your dowel, with room to attach it to the curtain. If it is too short, cut your tab strips longer.

6. Before attaching the tabs to the curtain, decide how far apart you want to space them. The optimal space between tabs depends on the fabric; try 4″ spacing and see if that amount works with your fabric, a stiffer fabric requires less space between tabs. Use dressmaker's chalk to mark spots (on the wrong side of the fabric) for each tab, beginning with a spot at each edge of the curtain panel, in the middle, and between the middle and sides. Then add marks in the space in between as needed.

7. Fold each tab strip in half and position **loop side down** on the marked places on the wrong side of the curtain, with raw edges of tab about ¼″ below top of curtain. Push one edge of each tab ¼″ forward of the other to eliminate as much bulk as possible, making it easier to sew and less likely to break the thread. Pin all the tabs in place.

8. Stitch in a straight line across all the tabs, crossing about ¼″ down from the raw edges.

9. Press each tab up with your fingers, pin, and stitch close to the top edge of the curtain, across all the turned-up tabs.

10. Slip the tabs on the dowels and hang. Pin up the hem so the bottom of the curtain is just ⅛″ from the inside bottom window casing.

11. Remove curtain from rod and stitch up hem.

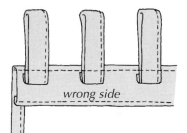

wrong side

To finish, press the tab loops up and stitch across all of them, close to the edge of the curtain.

Valances

Valances are often the answer to that finishing touch a window treatment needs. They are basically short curtains that run across the full width of the window. Valances can be used alone or in combination with longer drapes or curtains. There are construction techniques for making valances out of a variety of materials, producing a range of different styles and effects.

BALLOON VALANCE

Balloon valances are a great look and easy to make. They dress up a kitchen, are terrific in a bedroom, and can work just about anywhere else. They are a nuisance if you have to raise or lower them, so I prefer to use them as decorative treatments. You can use them for privacy, though, if you place them in the lower half of the window.

For a smashing effect, hang a balloon valance above a bed. You'll need a valance approximately 14″–16″ deep and a framework to attach it to — the railings of a tester bed or, perhaps, a homemade frame of 1″x2″ boards nailed to the ceiling. In all likelihood the studs beneath the Sheetrock or plaster of your ceiling will not be in a convenient position for you to nail directly into them. If you pound a nail in the location necessary to attach the frame boards and the nail does not grab into a stud, use a molly screw (directions on page 110).

A balloon valance is attached to the window by using the wide, approximately 2½″, metal curtain rods. A pocket to slide the rod is sewn into the top of the curtain. (See instructions on following page.) Before making curtains, purchase the rods and mount them.

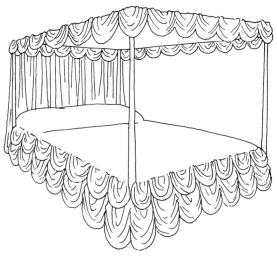

If you want to make your little girl feel as if she's sleeping on a cloud, make a balloon dust ruffle for the bottom of her bed and a valance balloon overhead. Finish with a balloon valance edging on the bedspread for a perfectly heavenly look.

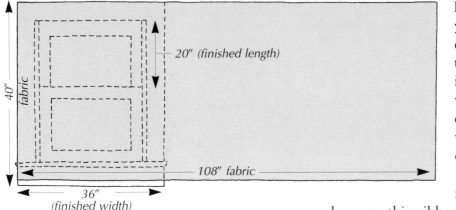

20″ (finished length)

40″ fabric

108″ fabric

36″
(finished width)

Believe it or not, you need this much fabric to create a valance for the window pictured above.

Determining fabric amount. Begin by measuring your window to figure out the desired finished dimensions of your valance. You will need fabric that is triple the finished width and double the finished length. For example, if your window is 36″ wide, you will need to sew widths of fabric together to achieve 3x36″=108″. And for a finished valance length of 20″, you will need a 40″ length of fabric.

Other materials. In addition to fabric, you will need ½″ to ¾″ bias tape (to make casing) and some cord or very thin ribbon (¼″). To calculate how much you'll need of each of these, you need to know how many casings you will have on the valance. The number of casings depends on the amount of fabric, the width of the window, and how scalloped you want the balloons to look. For our sample valance, you will have eight casings. So you will need 8x40″=320″, or 9 yards each of bias tape and cording. If you are not hanging the valance on a rod, you'll also need cord for the horizontal casing if you are attaching the valance to a wooden frame with Velcro or sewing it onto another piece of fabric, such as a bedspread, instead of using a curtain rod.

If you have never made balloon valances, you may want to practice this technique with an old bedsheet first.

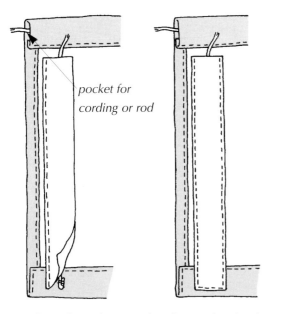

pocket for cording or rod

Attach cord to valance and enclose with strip of bias tape.

Instructions for Balloon Valance

1. Measure window, figure out desired finished size of valance, and cut (or assemble) a piece of fabric that is 3 times as wide and 2 times as long as finished dimensions (as described above).

2. Finish bottom edge of the fabric by turning fabric under ½″ and press. Turn edge under ½″ again and stitch. Finish side edges of fabric by turning under ½″ and press. Turn under again 1½″ and stitch. Finish top edge by turning fabric under ½″ and press. Turn under again 4″ and stitch. (If your rod is 2½″ wide, a 3″-wide pocket is necessary to allow rod to slide.) If desired, stitch 1″ from top folded edge of pocket to create a ruffled edge along top.

3. Position vertical strips of bias tape evenly along the wrong side of the fabric, beginning with strips ½″ from each side and one in the center, then adding additional strips as needed, approximately 12″ apart from each other. Pin bias strips at the top and bottom, turning the raw edges at top and bottom under and positioning top of tape to be about ¼″ below top hem, and bottom edge of tape to be ¼″ from bottom edge of fabric.

4. Sew the left side of each bias casing in place by stitching a straight line close to the edge.

5. Cut lengths of cord or ribbon for each casing, about 2″ longer than the casing itself. Position the bottom end of the cord inside the casing, about ¼″ above the bottom of the casing, as illustrated. Secure the cord by stitching it to the fabric, backstitching several times.

6. Sew a straight seam along the right-side edge of each casing, taking care not to catch the cording in the stitching.

7. To gather the valance lengthwise, pull each of the vertical cords until the fabric is evenly ruffled at the desired height. Secure the cords by backstitching across each one close to the top hemline. Cut off the excess cord.

8. If the valance is being mounted on a 2½″ rod, slip the rod through the top pocket, which will automatically gather the fabric.

9. If you are not using a rod to hang the valance, gather it width-wise, by cutting a piece of cording or ribbon that is 3″ longer than the width of the fabric. Stick a large safety pin through one end of the cord and draw it through the top hem pocket. Catch the other end of the cord just before it enters the pocket and secure it to the edge of the pocket by stitching and backstitching along the open side. Pull the cord through the other end of the pocket and gather the fabric along it to the desired width. Stitch along this end of the pocket securely. Stitch finished valance to another fabric or Velcro.

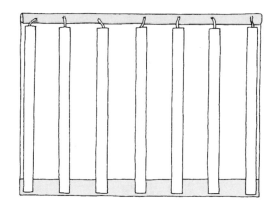

Evenly space vertical strips of bias tape across width of valance.

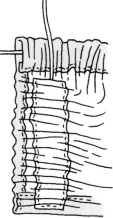

First gather vertical strips by pulling cords. Then gather the valance horizontally by either putting it on a rod or pulling a cord through the top pocket.

RUFFLED VALANCE

A ruffled valance is no more than a shortened café curtain. Valances vary in length, but are usually about 12″.

Determining fabric amount. You need a piece of fabric that is at least double the width of your window. If you want a very tight ruffle, use a piece up to three times the width of your window. Lengthwise, figure the amount of fabric needed according to the directions for the café curtain on page 88, allowing for a finished length of 12″, or whatever length you desire.

BOX-PLEATED VALANCE

A valance adds a finished look to drapery. Visually tying together the two panels of cloth hanging on either side of a window with a connector across the top creates a more pleasing flow, and a sense of the window as a complete unit. If you have floor-length drapes and would like valances (as long as they don't look too informal for your decorating style), a box-pleated valance is a great and simple solution.

A box-pleated valance can be hung over drapes or on a bed canopy.

While fabric is the most popular covering for wooden valance frames, there are many other options. Be creative in developing a covering that enhances the look and decor of your room. Here are a few alternative coverings I have tried.

- Large straw fans from India can be fastened onto a valance. The effect is straw matting in a curved design. It takes many staples to secure the matting; cover these with brown touch-up paint.

- Mirrors create a great effect on a valance. Attach 9"-wide mirrored strips to the valance front and sides with Liquid Nails and mastic. For added zip, purchase some striping (decorative stripes applied to cars for that custom look) at an auto parts store and edge the valance.

  One warning about using Liquid Nails: This product works so well that you get no second chances. So make sure all your measurements are correct before you apply it. You won't be able to move it again!

- For a wooden bathroom valance, try to copy the colors and pattern of the fabric used in an adjoining bedroom. Braided trim can be glued to the edge to further echo the fabric in the bedroom.

To mount a box-pleated valance, you first need to build a frame from 1"x2" boards. Either a box-pleated or ruffled valance can be attached (with Velcro) to this frame.

The box-pleated valance has a somewhat more polished look than a ruffled valance and is quite simple to make. You'll need about twice as much fabric as the finished length of the valance. For example, for a 7' finished valance, you will need at least 14' of fabric. For buying fabric, it's best to round up to the nearest even yard measurement, in this case 15' = 5 yards. Most finished valances are about 15" long. Depending on the desired length of your valance, you may be able to cut two lengths from one width of fabric. Allow extra fabric for matching a recurring pattern.

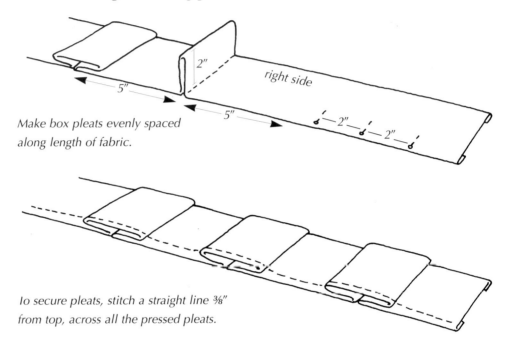

Make box pleats evenly spaced along length of fabric.

To secure pleats, stitch a straight line ⅜" from top, across all the pressed pleats.

Instructions for Box-Pleated Valance

1. Cut fabric into strips that are approximately 16" wide. Make narrow (⅜") hems on both long edges, turning the raw edges under, if desired.
2. The pleats will be 2" deep and 5" apart. On the right side of the fabric, begin by measuring 5 inches from one edge, then fold together 4 inches of fabric to make a 2"-deep pleat (on the right side of the fabric with wrong side of pleated fabric facing inward together). Pin at the top. Measure another 5 inches from the base of the first pleat to determine the correct fold for the 2nd pleat. Continue until you have pinned pleats along the full length of your fabric.
3. Stitch a straight line along the top of each pleat fold line.
4. On the right side of the fabric, press the pleats flat.

5. Stitch ⅜″ from the top of the valance, across all the pressed pleats.

6. Cut a strip of Velcro the same length as the valance and sew it close to the top edge of the valance (with a row of stitching on either side of the Velcro).

7. Staple an accompanying piece of Velcro to the wooden frame. Press the valance onto the frame. If you don't want to use Velcro, you can attach the valance to the frame with a hot glue gun, but this is best for a temporary arrangement.

PADDED FABRIC VALANCE

A padded wooden valance can be made to coordinate with the fabric and colors of your drapes or any other element in the room. First you need to make a wooden frame out of ½″ plywood. This can be a simple box shape or have curves in whatever shape or style you find pleasing. The sides should be about 6″ deep. You will need a width of fabric that measures about 10″ more than the total dimension of the three sides of your valance. The fabric should also be at least 10″ longer than the longest part of the valance (from top to bottom). You will also need some old towels for padding.

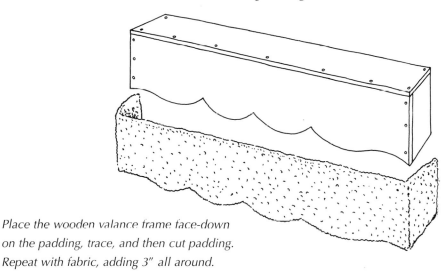

Place the wooden valance frame face-down on the padding, trace, and then cut padding. Repeat with fabric, adding 3″ all around.

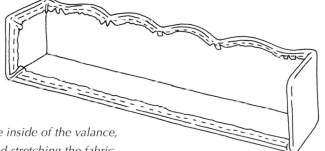

Staple the fabric to the inside of the valance, clipping the curves and stretching the fabric to keep the front smooth.

Instructions for a Padded Fabric Valance

1. Set the wood valance front side down on the towel. Trace around the valance, and then cut the toweling to fit exactly. If you need to use more than one towel, make sure the edges of the two pieces just meet but do not overlap (or they will create a lumpy look on the front).
2. Staple the toweling to the wooden valance.
3. Lay the padded valance face down on the wrong side of the fabric and trace around the valance. Draw a second line 3″ outside the first line to allow fabric for wrapping around the edges of the valance to the back. Cut along this outer line.
4. Starting at the middle front edges (upper, then lower) of the fabric, stretch the fabric around the edge of the valance and staple on the inside. Clip the fabric as needed to keep the fabric on the front of the valance smooth. This can be tricky. Straight edges are very easy; curved edges are a little more challenging. The trick is to clip into the fabric at the the inside corners almost to the edge of the wood and then stretch the fabric. It often takes three or more clips to get around an inside curve.
5. Nail a small metal bracket to each end of the valance to attach it to the wall. Simple bracket hangers are available at hardware stores and can be secured to the window frame with a nail or molly screw.

WOODEN VALANCES

I have found wooden valances to be an especially great asset in the bathroom. One of the tricks I've developed for mounting inexpensive, yet up-style looking bathroom lighting is to position a wooden valance over the bathroom sink, projecting about 12″ from the wall, and fasten a strip of incandescent lights to the backside of the valance. (See photo at left.) The lighting strips cost only $12 to $20, eliminating the need to buy expensive bathroom fixtures. Using this concealed lighting setup also allows room for mounting mirrors on the entire wall surface over the sink. If you have walls of 2x4 construction on either side of the sink counter, you can also add built-in his/hers medicine cabinets on either side of the mirrors. This is a simple job for a carpenter or even a do-it-yourselfer. For directions on making built-in wall cabinets, see the built-in shelving unit on page 114.

A wooden valance over a bathroom sink provides an attractive cover for inexpensive, yet effective, strip lighting.

Wooden valances also provide an elegant way to hide your shower curtain rod. Moldings added along the top and/or bottom make an attractive detail.

LENGTHENING A SHOWER CURTAIN

If you raise your shower curtain bar to hide behind a valance, you may find that your fabric shower curtain is too short. If you've got a sewing machine, it's fairly simple to extend the length. Here's how.

1. Measure the height from your new shower rod position to just above the shower basin. Measure your shower curtain and figure the inches you need to add to meet the new height. Add 2" to this amount (for seam allowances).
2. Using the measurement determined in step 1, cut a strip from one side of the curtain.
3. Measure 3" below the holes at the top of the shower curtain, draw a horizontal line across the curtain, and cut off the strip of holes along this line. Set it aside.
4. Pin the strip of fabric cut from the side of the curtain to the top of the curtain, with right sides together and raw edges even. Trim the strip to be even with the curtain width. Stitch together with a ⅝" seam. Press seam open.
5. Pin the top strip of holes to the top of the curtain, right sides together with raw edges even. Stitch together with a ⅝" seam. Press seam open.
6. Press long, unfinished side of curtain under (turning raw edge under, if desired) and stitch ⅝" from edge.

Rods and Hardware for Window Treatments

Even if you've never installed anything using a hammer, screws, and nails, you can learn to put up the hardware for window treatments. With a few tools and a few tips you're on your way.

You should be familiar with several different mounting systems, including the traverse rod, standard stationary flat rod, dowel rod (mounted outside casing), and dowel rod (mounted inside casing).

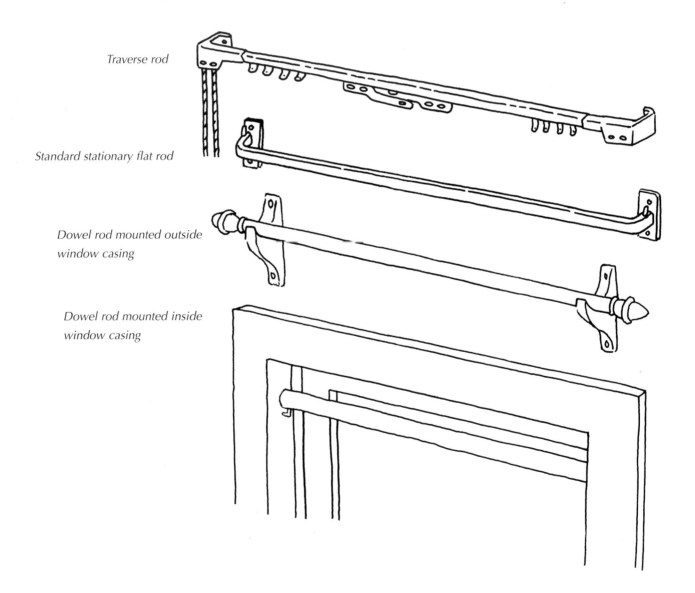

Traverse rod

Standard stationary flat rod

Dowel rod mounted outside window casing

Dowel rod mounted inside window casing

TRAVERSE RODS

Traverse rods allow you to easily open and close drapes. When used on a picture window or patio door, the rod should be positioned outside the window casing to accommodate the massive volume of fabric when the drapes are opened and avoid blocking the light. For a 6′ window, extend the rod 12″ beyond the window casing. Use molly screws to mount the rod (see page 110). Traverse rods vary in design; follow the installation instructions that come with your particular style rod.

STANDARD STATIONARY FLAT CURTAIN RODS

These inexpensive metal rods come in a variety of widths and lengths and are quite simple to install (see installation instructions included with your rod). The installation usually requires only small nails or screws, which are provided with the rod.

DOWEL RODS (OUTSIDE CASING)

For a few dollars you can buy wooden curtain holders that can be mounted with two screws on either side of the window casing. Then you can cut a dowel to fit these holders, allowing the rod to extend 4″–6″ beyond the rod holder at each end. There are also a wide variety of decorative rods available with fancy finials on the ends, if that fits your style.

DOWEL RODS (INSIDE CASING)

Dowel rods mounted inside your window casing are about the most inexpensive (and unobtrusive) way to hang a tab curtain.

Instructions for Mounting an Inside-Casing Wooden Dowel Rod
1. Purchase a dowel 1″ in diameter and long enough to fit inside the window casing. Purchase two 1″ L-shaped hooks with a screw end.
2. Screw a hook to each upper inside edge of the window casing (about 1½″ from the top) so the hook projects out toward the middle of the window and there is enough space for the dowel (when hole is drilled) to sit on top of it. Be sure the hooks are evenly spaced from the top on both sides. To install the hook, I usually take my trusty hammer and give it a couple of hard smacks and then turn it by hand as far as I can. Or, you can insert the hooks by turning with pliers.

Installing a Dowel Rod Inside Casing

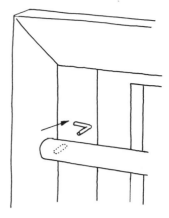

1. *Line up drilled hole in dowel with L-shaped hook.*

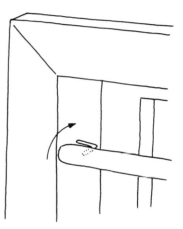

2. *Slide dowel onto hook and rotate up.*

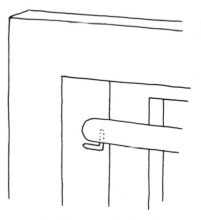

3. *Dowel rod rests neatly inside window casing.*

ADDING A BOTTOM RUFFLE

Bottom ruffles can be added to many of your fabric decorating creations — café curtains, round tablecloths, and bedspreads. Ruffles can range from 4″ to 16″ in length, depending on the look you want.

To make the ruffle, you can either use a ruffler attachment on your sewing machine (if you have one) or gather the material by hand. When using a ruffler, first do a test run on a scrap piece of the same fabric to gauge how much material you're going to use and how tight the ruffles will be. To do this, create a 12″ length of ruffle and cut off excess from the sides. Then rip out the ruffles and measure the length of fabric you used to make those 12″ of ruffles. Multiply this amount by the number of feet of ruffles you need, and you'll know what length piece of fabric to start with.

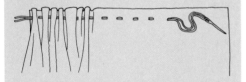

If you don't have a ruffler, you can do the gathering by hand with double thread and a simple running stitch. Don't make your line of stitching any longer than 1 yard, and be sure to knot the thread securely before you start. Once you've adjusted the ruffles, secure the thread by stitching over both ends with machine or handmade running stitches.

3. Measure the length between the two sides of the window casings where the hooks are mounted. Cut the dowel rod ¼″ shorter than this.

4. Turn the L-hooks halfway down (so the hook is pointing out). Hold the dowel up to the hooks and mark the spot at each end where the dowel meets the hook.

5. Drill a hole slightly larger than the diameter of the L-hook at each of the marked points. You'll need a battery-operated drill and an assortment of drill bits for this job.

6. Slide the curtains on to the dowel and then set the dowel on the hooks — they should slip on fairly easily — and with both hands push the entire dowel up, so the hooks are pointing up.

Other Fabric Decorating Projects

I am continually discovering new ways to use basic sewing skills in home decorating projects. A number of projects have been described in Chapter 3 on window treatments. Here are a few more suggestions for other easy projects that are most useful.

BED DUST RUFFLE

Dust ruffles on a bed create a distinctive look and fit beautifully with certain styles. A bed without a dust ruffle tends to look sleeker, simpler, more contemporary, and somewhat more masculine. A bed with a dust ruffle looks cozier, although, depending on the fabric, it can also look elegant. One of the best things about dust ruffles is that they make possible a whole new dimension for storage: under-the-bed storage boxes or drawers are easily hidden. Dust ruffles are simple to make.

Determining fabric amount. The total fabric length you'll need depends on how tightly gathered a look you want. The distance around a double bed is approximately 6 yards; 12 yards of fabric makes a moderately gathered dust ruffle and 18 yards makes a very full one.

To calculate the amount of fabric you need for a ruffle, you will need to know the width of the fabric you are purchasing and the height of your bed. For example, say your fabric is 48″ wide and your bed is high, requiring a 22″ ruffle. Add 1″ to allow for your gathering lines and 1″ for hemming, making for a total of 24″ for the length of fabric needed for your ruffle. This measurement, 24″, is half of 48″, the width of the fabric, so you can cut two lengths of ruffle from every yard of fabric. Therefore, 6 yards of 48″ fabric will make a 12-yard ruffle (enough for a moderate gather) and 9 yards will make an 18-yard ruffle (enough for a very full gather).

For a contemporary or very tailored look, you can actually make a dust ruffle without a gather, by simply attaching straight fabric to the sheet cover. This look works best with a heavy upholstery fabric and added trim (such as cording or fringe) along the bottom edge.

Instructions for a Dust Ruffle

1. On the bed frame you'll be covering, measure the distance from the floor to the edge of the mattress cover. Add 2″ for seam allowances. Add additional inches if you want the ruffle to hang on the floor or if you desire a deeper hem.

2. Cut the ruffle fabric into long strips in the width determined in step 1; stitch all the strips together to make one long strip that is at least twice as long as the total circumference of the mattress (see guidelines in box at left). Turn the edge along one long side of the strip under and sew a 1″ hem.

3. Gather the upper edge of the ruffle strip using a ruffler on your sewing machine. I recommend testing the gathering on a scrap piece of fabric first to get just the right tightness of gathers.

4. Remove the mattress from the bed and place an old flat bed sheet on the box spring. Using a pencil, mark the edges of the box spring on the sheet. Remove the sheet and make another line 2″ out from the one already marked. Cut along this line.

5. With right sides together, pin the ruffle to the sheet along three sides, keeping raw edges even. Stitch together 2″ from the edge of the sheet.

6. Place the cover on the box spring, arrange the ruffle, and replace the mattress on top.

Alternative Method: Instead of making a sheet cover, attach the dust ruffle directly to the edge of the box spring mattress with Velcro strips. Sew a narrow (½″) strip of Velcro onto the top edge of the finished dust ruffle. Using a hot-glue gun, glue strips of Velcro to the top rim of your box spring mattress.

This method makes it easy to remove the ruffle for laundering or simply a change. You can also use Velcro to attach a valance around a tester or canopy bed, or a skirt for your laundry tubs or dressing table.

DRESSING TABLE SKIRT

Dressing tables are regaining popularity, and rightly so. They are useful, and they can fit in with any decor. My mother made one for me when I was about six years old. It was child-sized and kidney-shaped with a pink satin skirt. We didn't have much money, but because of my mother's sewing ability, sitting at my dressing table made me feel like a princess.

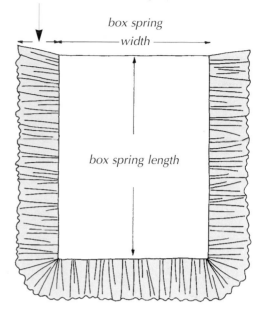

distance from bottom edge of mattress to floor

box spring width

box spring length

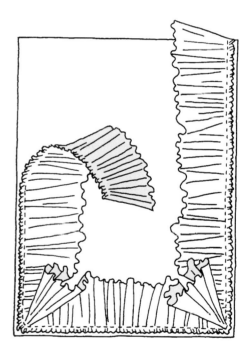

Attaching dust ruffle to flat bed sheet.

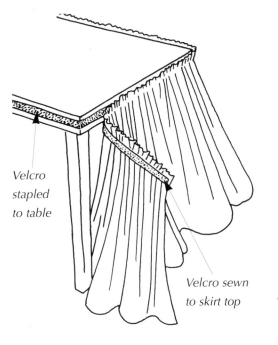

Velcro stapled to table

Velcro sewn to skirt top

Instructions for Dressing Table Skirt

1. Decide what kind of skirt you want: pleated or ruffled. If ruffled, decide what degree of gathering you want: moderate or very full.
2. Measure the length from the top of the table edge (where the skirt will be attached) to the floor. Add 2″ to this measurement: This is the width of fabric you will need.
3. Measure the total circumference of the sides of the table you plan to cover. For a cap pleated skirt, follow the directions for determining fabric length and pleating on page 94. For a ruffled skirt, follow the directions for making a dust ruffle for a bed on page 101.
4. Sew a strip of Velcro onto the upper edge of the skirt. Staple the related strip of Velcro to the table edge. Attach the skirt to the table.

TABLECLOTHS

Floor-length tablecloths add visual impact to a room. Even if you like the appearance of your tabletop surface, it's worth making a covering for those times when you want a change of look and a dash of color. If your room has a monochromatic color scheme (e.g., a color scheme in all the same colors or hue), try a tablecloth in a stronger shade in the same color family, or in a contrasting color. One interesting combination is a striped tablecloth in a room decorated in a floral pattern, or vice versa. Another possibility is to use the same fabric in both a window treatment and a tablecloth and to position the two closely as a unit.

To make a square or rectangular tablecloth that will be used frequently, try using a large no-iron sheet (often found at an inexpensive price in discount stores). A queen- or king-sized sheet can often eliminate extra seaming. It is most important, however, that you find find just the right fabric pattern and color to fit in with your decor, seams or not.

PIECING AND MATCHING TABLECLOTH FABRIC

There should never be a seam running down the middle of the tablecloth. To avoid this, you may have to cut a center panel in the full width of the fabric, and then cut two separate strips of fabric to be joined on either side of the center panel to get your final desired width.

If you are using a fabric with a recognizable pattern, such as a horizontal stripe, buy 1 extra yard of fabric and adjust the pattern to meet before cutting the side panels (as illustrated).

Instructions for Square or Rectangular Tablecloth

1. Starting at the center of the table, measure the table across half its width and then down to the floor where you want the hem to be. Double that measurement and write it down. Repeat this process for the length, measuring from the center of the table again. Add 2" to each of these measurements for hemming allowances.

2. To determine the amount of fabric needed, it helps to draw a diagram and write in your measurements. Then, you need to know the width of the fabric you've selected. For example, say the total length you arrived at in step 1 is 121" and the width is 85". The fabric you have selected is 60" wide. Divide 36" (1 yard) into 121" (the total length) and you arrive at 3½ yards (rounded up to the nearest quarter yard) as the length of fabric you will need. However, since the width of fabric needed is more than 60", you will need two lengths each 3½ yards long, for a total of 7 yards of 60" fabric.

3. If you are sewing several strips of fabric together to obtain the final width, add in ¾" for each seam allowance before cutting your fabric. Sew the seams together by making a flat-felled seam. To do this, stitch the two edges together in a ¾" seam. Press the seam to one side, turning and pressing the raw edges under together, flat against the tablecloth fabric. Stitch the seam to the tablecloth. This eliminates the raw selvage and adds extra durability.

4. If you have any leftover fabric, make matching cloth napkins simply by cutting squares and making tiny rolled hems around all 4 edges. A nice size for a napkin is approximately 20" square.

Instructions for a Round Tablecloth

1. Measure the length of the table you want to cover, beginning in the center of the table and measuring from that point to the edge of the table and continuing down to the floor. Double this measurement and add 2" to allow for a 1" hem all around.

2. If the total length you arrive at is greater than the width of your selected fabric, join several strips of fabric to achieve the desired length. As described in step 3 above for the rectangular tablecloth, try to avoid having a unattractive seam down the center of the tablecloth. Instead, piece the fabric, as illustrated on opposite page.

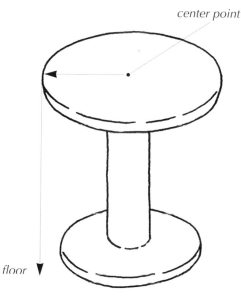

center point

floor

To measure the length of the table, begin at the center point and go down to the floor.

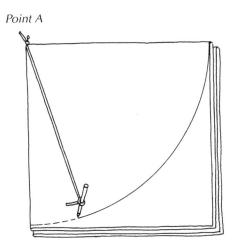

Point A

Use a pencil attached to a piece of string to draw the circular cutting line for a round tablecloth.

3. Once you have a piece of fabric that measures the desired length, fold this piece in half and then in half again to form a square (with wrong side out). Cut a piece of string equal in length to the measurement from the center of the table to the floor (as figured in step 1). Tie a pen or pencil to one end of the string. Have someone hold the end of the string at Point A while you move the tied pen across the fabric, marking a circular outline (see illustration).

4. Cut along the marked line. Unfold the fabric. You should have a fairly round circle that you can then hem or add a ruffle or cording to around the bottom edge.

MAKING FABRIC-COVERED CORDING

Cording helps keep the bottom of a round tablecloth flared out, whether or not you attach it to a ruffle. You'll find cording in many diameters. For a large tablecloth, ½" looks particularly nice.

To make cording that matches the tablecloth fabric, you can buy unfinished cording, which is simply wrapped cotton batting, and cover it. To do this:

1. Measure the total outer circumference of your cut table cloth and cut a piece of cording the same length.

2. Cut strips of fabric, on the bias if possible, with a width measurement equal to the circumference of the cording plus 1½". You will need enough strips to equal the length of your cording, plus several inches seam allowance.

3. Join the strips together by pinning right sides together (as illustrated) and stitching a ⅜" seam.

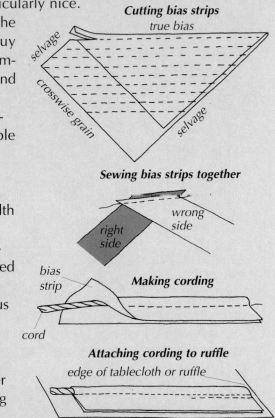

Cutting bias strips
true bias
selvage
crosswise grain
selvage

Sewing bias strips together
wrong side
right side

bias strip
Making cording
cord

Attaching cording to ruffle
edge of tablecloth or ruffle

4. Wrap the fabric strip around the cording, raw edges even and right side out. Use a zipper foot on your sewing machine to stitch close to the cording, enclosing it in the fabric.

5. Pin the covered cording to the bottom edge of the tablecloth (right sides together with raw edges even) and stitch. Trim seam and press up toward tablecloth on back.

FABRIC WALL COVERING

Fabric on your walls may be just the thing to finish off the look of a particular room. To do this, you will need a pair of very sharp scissors, a large (1-gallon-sized) container of premixed Border glue, a 4"-wide paintbrush, a utility knife, a ladder, thumbtacks, a long table, and some patience.

The walls should be at least primed; primed and painted is better. Any imperfections in the wall surface will show up as bumps on the finished face of the fabric, and any patchy or uneven color will show through on light background colors. So the smoother and more evenly colored you can make it, the better the result will be.

Determining fabric amount. It takes a considerable amount of fabric to cover an average-sized room, so take cost into consideration when you make the decision to use fabric on walls.

To determine the amount of fabric necessary measure the width and height of each wall you plan to cover. Convert the width measurement to inches in order to compare it to the width of the fabric. For example, if the width of your wall is 12', that equals 144". If the fabric you plan to use is 54", divide 54" into 144": the result is 2.67, which means you will need approximately 2⅔ widths of fabric. This number is close enough to round up to 3 widths for the 12' wall.

Now, consider the height of the room. Say the height of our sample room is 8'. Add an extra 12" for cutting and trimming allowances: That makes a total height allowance of 9', or 3 yards. Since we know we need 3 widths of fabric this length to cover the wall in questions, we multiply 3 by 3 yards, to arriave at a total of 9 yards of fabric needed to cover this 8' by 12' wall.

Say, we want to cover the whole room, and this room is 12' square with two windows and two doors. First, we multiply 9 yards (the amount needed for 1 wall) by 4 walls, for a total of 36 yards of fabric to cover the whole room. While you could subtract a bit of yardage to allow for the windows and doors, I don't recommend doing so. It is better to have a little extra fabric than to find yourself running just shy of the needed amount. Don't forget that, just as with wallpaper, if you're using a fabric with a repeating horizontal pattern, you need to allow extra fabric to be sure you can match the pattern.

Fabric is applied to the wall with basically the same techniques used for applying wallpaper. Before beginning, invest in a truly sharp pair of scissors.

Instructions for Fabric Wall Covering

1. Drop a plumb line from the ceiling to the floor and draw a vertical guideline down the wall with a light pencil line. If there is a pattern design on the fabric, determine what part of the design you want next to the ceiling line.

2. Using sharp scissors, cut a piece of fabric that is 5" to 7" longer than your wall length. Cut off the selvage edges of each length

of fabric just as you're preparing to apply it. (If you do it earlier, the edges will fray.) It is nearly impossible to cut your strip at precisely the right length because the ceiling line is usually off just a bit, so you need a little leeway for adjusting the fabric pattern and edges to line up.

3. With the brush, apply glue to the area of the wall where you're applying the length of fabric. Carefully attach the fabric to the wall, working from the top down. Fabric stretches when moistened by glue so work quickly to keep the pattern straight. Try to avoid repositioning the fabric by pulling it off the wall, as this might peel the paint off as well.

4. When the pattern is straight, smooth out the fabric with your hands or a damp towel. Begin at the center of the fabric strip and work out to both ends, pressing down smoothly. Crease the fabric at the top and bottom with the wallpaper knife. Pull the edges back slightly and cut with the scissors (usually fabric cannot be cut with a utility knife). Smooth the fabric back down.

5. Prepare the next length of fabric and apply glue to the wall. If you need to match a pattern in the fabric, begin applying the new strip about halfway down the wall where the pattern matches. Then work up to the top and down to the bottom from there.

6. Going around corners, you may have to split the fabric halfway up the wall and insert a piece in the corner and then smooth the fabric on each split side. This is necessary because walls aren't straight.

Basic Woodworking, Refinishing, and Tiling Techniques

Almost as soon as you have your first decorating idea, the thought will occur to you, "I can do this myself." You can save a lot of money by doing the basic decorating and renovation work yourself: from hanging curtain rods to installing molding and tile to building cabinets. With just a few tools and a little knowledge, you will be surprised at how much you can accomplish and how much satisfaction you will derive.

Woodworking

Building projects range from the very simple to the complex jobs that require skilled work done by a professional carpenter. But you can handle easy jobs like hanging curtain rods, mounting basic shelving, and even putting down wide pine board floors.

Basic Tools

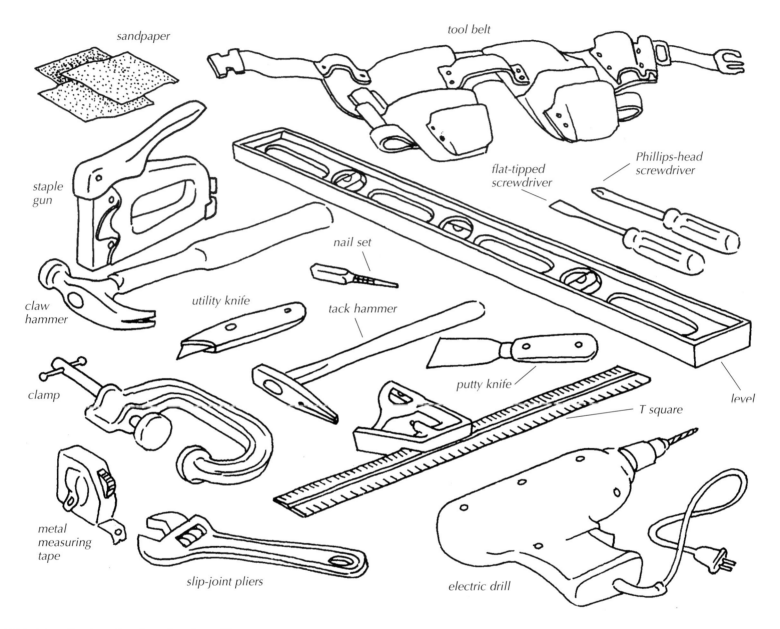

sandpaper

tool belt

staple gun

flat-tipped screwdriver

Phillips-head screwdriver

nail set

claw hammer

utility knife

tack hammer

clamp

putty knife

level

T square

metal measuring tape

slip-joint pliers

electric drill

With this collection of tools on hand, you'll be ready to take on most simple decorating projects.

The most common projects do-it-yourselfer home decorators face have to do with attaching something to a wall, whether it's a curtain rod, a towel rod, or a shelf and doing maintenance repairs. For these tasks, you'll need the following basic set of tools.

Pliers. Slip-joint pliers to remove nails or brads and to hold a nut while you are turning a bolt.

Handsaw. This tool is classified by the number of teeth it has. I prefer a jig saw for home use; it is electric and priced less than $40.00.

Clamps. You should have three different sizes on hand — 2″, 4″, 6″ — for holding pieces together while gluing.

Utility knife. For cutting Sheetrock, cardboard, and other stick materials.

Claw hammer. A 12–13 oz one works well for pounding or pulling out large nails.

Tack hammer. For inserting tacks and small nails.

Large T square. A metal one that's 48″ in length for laying out precise photo arrangements, cutting out fabric, and marking lumber to be cut.

Level. Useful for installing anything of length that needs to be level, such as curtain rods.

Nail set. For countersinking nails.

Putty knife. For applying taping compound in holes or repairing nail holes.

Staple gun. For covering valances with padding and fabric.

Coping saw. For trimming out molding cuts.

Miter box. For cutting angles for moldings.

Electric drill. For drilling holes in Sheetrock and/or plaster.

Flat-tipped and Phillips-head screwdrivers. Large and small.

Sandpaper. Assorted grits.

Flexible metal measuring tape.

Tool belt.

DEVELOPING YOUR SKILLS

If you find that you like using a hammer and nails, you might consider taking an adult education class in woodworking. It can be extremely rewarding to learn basic woodworking terms and procedures and learn how to use tools properly and safely, all in just five to ten class sessions. It is amazing what you can do when you know how to select the right tools for a job and feel confident about using them. Even if your skill never extends beyond simple household repairs, it's worth acquiring the basic tools and learning how to use them.

If you're faced with a number of home improvement projects, you might find it useful to invest in a set of how-to woodworking books. I purchased a set published by Time/Life Books (see "Further Reading") about ten years ago and they have proven to be invaluable to me. I've even had carpenters working on my jobs ask to refer to particular information in these books. Even if you don't plan on doing the work yourself, reading these books will give you a better understanding of what's involved in the work to be done. Moreover, when you do decide to attempt projects, you'll have a step-by-step guide to help you.

If you have a towel rack or other object that keeps pulling out of the wall, a molly screw can solve the problem.

There are many different kinds and sizes of molly screws. You can buy the screw and the anchor separately or together. To install molly screws you need a drill and drill bits, hammer, and screwdriver.

To install a molly screw:

1. Drill a hole into the wall the size of the anchor or slightly smaller.

2. Lightly tap the anchor into the hole so it's even with the wall surface.

3. Insert the screw and tighten to spread the casing in back. Remove the screw and put it through the item you are hanging and screw it into the casing or put the screw back into the casing, allowing a little of the screw head to project and hang the object from it.

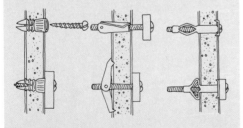

Three different styles of molly screws that are useful for hanging heavy objects on Sheetrock or plaster walls are (left to right): anchor, toggle bolt, molly bolt.

More Advanced Building Projects

If you're interested in taking on more complex construction projects such as building a closet or divider or compartments for a closet, installing shelves or molding, or building radiator covers, you're going to need some tools in additional to those listed above. This is my suggested project tool kit:

- Adjustable wrench (adjustable for different-sized nuts)
- Round and half-round files
- Pry bar
- Locking grip pliers
- Wood chisel (necessary for installing inset hinges)
- Hacksaw
- Block plane for trimming end grain
- Jack plane for trimming along the grain
- Circular saw
- Saber saw
- Spiral ratchet screwdriver
- Ball peen hammer
- Whetstone

A tool bench is wonderful to have but not absolutely necessary. However, you will need a container to keep all the smaller tools together while you are working with them. An empty five-gallon taping-compound bucket works well. (There are aprons available that fit around the outsides of these buckets with lots of pockets to put smaller items in.) With your bucket and tool belt, you'll be ready for any situation. There is nothing so inconvenient and aggravating as getting to the top of a ladder all poised to mark where the molly screw goes, only to discover that you forgot a pencil. With a tool belt, you'll always have the necessary tools literally within arm's reach.

Mark every tool you own with a dab of brightly colored paint or fingernail polish so it doesn't get mixed up with someone else's.

Building Corner Shelves

A simple corner shelf can be made by fastening strips of narrow molding to adjoining sides of the wall with finishing nails, and then cutting a shelf that fits on these moldings. Because of the configuration of a corner, no other securing factor is necessary.

To build one corner shelf 23" in depth, you will need:

- One #2 pine board (1" thick x 12" wide and 6' in length)
- 4' of ½" pine molding
- 2" finishing nails
- Jigsaw and punch
- Yardstick
- Hammer
- Level
- A couple yards of string

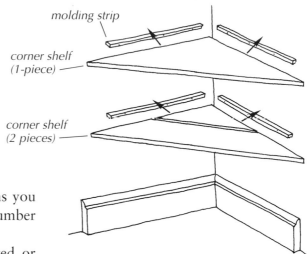

Corner shelves can be easily made that sit on top of strips of narrow molding mounted on the adjoining corner walls.

With a jigsaw, you can easily cut the boards to whatever dimensions you need. Remember that the stated dimensions of boards purchased from lumber stores are *not* true dimensions, a 1x6 actually measures about ¾"x5½".

Number 2 pine boards are fairly smooth and can be either painted or stained. This grade of wood is likely to have some knots in it so, if you plan to paint it, seal the knot holes with a product such as BIN before applying paint. Just dab this product on the knots only.

Instructions for Corner Shelf

1. Determine the desired height of the shelf and mark that level on corner of the wall.
2. Determine the desired width (where the edges of the shelf will come out to on the corner walls) and mark that spot on the wall.
3. With the level draw a horizontal line to the point of the desired width and draw a line. Do this for both sides of the shelf.
4. Cut two strips of pine molding, each 2½" shorter than the length of the final shelf width (as drawn on the wall).
5. Place one strip of molding about 1½" from the inner corner, with the top of the molding lined up with the level line drawn on the wall. Nail it in place. Repeat on the other side with the remaining strip of molding.
6. Place one end of a piece of string on the outer left side of the shelf line; holding that end in place, stretch the other end to the outer right side and mark this place on the string. Measure the distance marked on the string. This is the finished front-edge length measurement of the shelf.
7. Cut a rectangular piece of shelf board that is the same length as the finished front-edge measurement. Cut the sides at a 45° angle to fit the corner. The finished shelf should fit snugly in the corner of the wall, resting on top of the molding strips. If you have to piece the board, you can cut a triangular piece for the rear of the shelf, as illustrated.

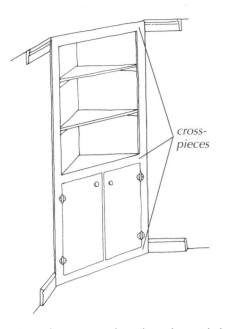

cross-pieces

A mock corner cupboard can be made by building a frame around corner shelves and adding doors. (See instructions at right.)

BUILDING A MOCK CORNER CUPBOARD

If you have a free corner in the dining room and would like to display your good dishes or a treasured collection, but can't spend the money to buy a new corner cupboard, you can make one!

A mock corner cupboard is simply a number of simple corner shelves with molding surrounding the shelves and two doors on a base.

You will need the following materials:

- Five #2 pine boards (1″ deep x 12″ wide and 6′ in length)
- 20′ of ½″ pine molding
- 2″ finishing nails
- Jigsaw and punch
- Yardstick
- Hammer
- Level
- A couple yards of string
- 1x4 boards to form the sides and three crosspieces for the cupboard
- Pair of premade doors
- 4 hinges
- 2 knobs

Instructions for Mock Corner Cupboard

1. Make corner shelves, as directed in previous section.
2. Measure the finished height of the cupboard, and cut two lengths of 1x4 board, each equal to this measurement.
3. Place each board perpendicular to one side of the shelves, flat against the shelving and with the edge of the board against the wall edge. Nail the boards to the shelves. Countersink the nail holes so that you can fill them in.
4. Carefully measure the width between the two side boards at the top, bottom, and middle, where the crosspieces will go. Mark this length with a metal T square along a 1x4 board three times. Cut precisely so the crosspieces will butt up against the side pieces.
5. Place each crosspiece level across the front of the shelves and attach by nailing through to the shelves.
6. To attach the doors to the bottom I suggest purchasing premade doors from a lumber store. Use hinges that are face mounted with screws. Face mounted means you do not have to cut hinges in with a chisel. If the premade door is too large, it can be trimmed down by cutting and sanding.
7. Add the knobs. (Knobs are usually installed by drilling a hole just slightly larger than the screw and twisting the knob on.) If desired, you can install doors on the top section of the cupboard as well.

HOW MANY 1x4 BOARDS ARE NEEDED?

You will need two lengths of board equal to the height of the cupboard. For example, if the desired finished height of your cupboard is 8', you will need double that measurement, or 16' for the two vertical sides of the cupboard.

For the crosspieces, first measure the total desired width of the finished cabinet. Subtract 4" from each end (or 8" total) from this width to account for the measurement of the two side boards. So if the total width of your cupboard is 32", you will need a 24" board for each crosspiece. Multiply that by 3 (the number of crosspieces), and the total would be 72", or 6'.

Add together the length required for the crosspieces and the vertical pieces: in this case, 16' plus 6' = 22' total required. It is important to purchase 1x4 boards in long lengths so that you do not have to piece any of the framing. In this case, two 12' pieces and one 6' piece will work well.

This mock corner cupboard was made by installing corner shelves, edging them with molding, and enclosing the bottom half with one door. The glass door on top was recycled from another cupboard in the house.

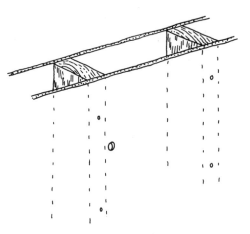

Find the 2 x 4 studs behind the wall board and draw vertical lines along the studs.

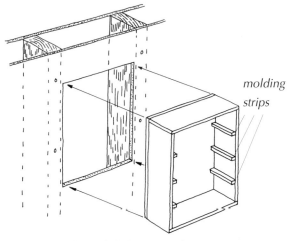

molding strips

Position the framed shelving unit between the studs.

Finish the edges of the unit by applying molding to the wall on all 4 sides.

MAKE A BUILT-IN SPICE RACK OR MEDICINE CABINET

If you have some wall space in the kitchen or bathroom, or if you are putting up new Sheetrock, you might want to consider building an in-the-wall shelving unit between two studs. This unit makes a great spice rack or medicine cabinet.

To make the spice rack, you will need:

- ■ Serrated handsaw
- ■ Sheetrock knife
- ■ Metal T square
- ■ Scraps of 1x4 lumber
- ■ Scraps of plywood
- ■ Scraps of ½″ molding
- ■ Shelves made from glass or boards 1″ thick

Instructions for Built-in Shelving Unit

1. Find studs by tapping along the wall until you come to a spot that sounds solid (or buy a stud finder at a hardware store). Mark the stud locations with vertical lines.

2. Draw two horizontal lines on the wall between studs to mark the desired finished size of the spice rack or medicine cabinet. Make sure the lines are level. (The eye can fool you, especially if your floor or ceiling isn't perfectly level.) Use a level for accuracy.

3. Hammer a large nail into the wall just inside one of the studs and pull it out, making a hole. Use this hole as a starting point to insert a serrated handsaw.

4. Using the studs as your guideline, cut Sheetrock on the marked horizontal lines, being careful not to remove any more than necessary or to cut through to Sheetrock on the other side. Then cut long vertical lines using a utility knife to cut the corners.

5. Measure the outside dimension of the hole you have cut, and make a frame from 1x4 boards with the same outside dimensions. Cover the back of the frame with a piece of plywood.

6. Cut short (3″) strips of ½″ molding to make shelf supports. Mark the desired height of shelves within this box, spaced to accommodate the height of your spice jars or medicine bottles. Nail molding strips on opposite sides of inside frame (as illustrated) to hold the shelves, making sure the two sides are level. Insert framed box into wall. Slide in shelves.

7. To create a finished look on the outside wall, apply molding around the 4 corner edges of the frame. L-shaped molding works well; cut the 4 corners at a 45° angle with a miter box so they fit snugly. If you don't have a miter box, simply do butt joints.

8. Paint or stain the unit to match your decor. For enclosing a medicine cabinet, you can add an unfinished pine door.

Hiring a Carpenter

Sometimes the most practical solution for getting a particular project done is to hire a carpenter. A week's worth of finish work by a skilled carpenter can be the most worthwhile investment you will make. For instance, say you are desperately short on closet space and you have a square kitchen with six doors and three windows and no wall space. You could hire a carpenter to frame out two closets (you have the room), Sheetrock and hang sliding doors on them, install closet rods and shelves to maximize storage space, and build a divider. It makes more sense to pay a carpenter and take care of your basic long-term needs than to buy a new piece of furniture for storage.

QUESTIONS TO ASK

Don't be afraid to shop around for a carpenter who is reputable and can do the job within your budget. Begin by asking people who have used a particular carpenter how satisfied they are with the work, and, if possible, go look at the work yourself. In your initial meeting with a carpenter, be sure to cover the following topics. (Note: These are good questions for plumbers and electricians as well.)

- State what the job entails. Make scale drawings on graph paper to show him or her (and be accurate with your measurements). If you have decided on particular products and materials, specify.
- Ask what the hourly rate is or get a quote on the total job.
- Ask for a time estimate for accomplishing each part of the job.
- Find out exactly what materials will be needed for the job and ask how you can save time and money by getting these yourself before the carpenter begins the work.

To save money, plan on doing all clean-up work yourself. Why pay the carpenter when you can do that? Besides, you learn a great deal by taking a close look at the work as you clean up. You might notice a missing detail that can be corrected before it is too late.

Painting and Refinishing Projects

For furniture refinishing and indoor painting jobs you will need some specific tools. Two indispensable items are a sander (reciprocating hand-held type) and a ladder. You can find good descriptions of basic painting and refinishing techniques in the product brochures provided at the paint store.

This "distressed-look" cabinetry, and refrigerator front were created with paint and stain, at a fraction of the cost of readymade custom cabinets.

CREATING DISTRESSED-LOOK CABINETS

One of the latest "hot" styles in custom kitchen cabinetry is new cupboards that have the look of aged, distressed wood. This is accomplished with a specialty paint job done in mellow-hued tones of traditional colors. The paint appears to be worn off around the handles, corners, and other places where wear would naturally occur.

I priced a set of this style cupboards in a well-known brand for a small kitchen I was designing; the cost exceeded $13,000. Granted, the interiors of these cabinets are well constructed out of solid wood, but what the consumer is really paying for is the specialized outside look. Rather than pay this much, I decided to duplicate the look on unfinished pine cabinets which I painted on-site. The cost of the unfinished cabinets for this kitchen came to around $2,000; the cost of labor for the paint job was about $750. There were additional costs to the homeowner for installation, hardware, and materials for painting.

To produce the aged effect that is key to this look, a stain is applied over a base-paint color. Selecting the right base-paint color is the most difficult part of this technique since the stain dulls the color down significantly. So the initial paint color will necessarily be much brighter than the finished look. The homeowner whose kitchen I designed chose a tone of blue that blended with the Dutch grayish-white blue in the kitchen's crackled tile design. When initially applied, the base color blue was extremely bright, even garish.

To get the right color with this technique, you really have to experiment on wood scraps first, starting out with a bright paint color and then trying out different color stains over it. In place of stain, you might also try using burnt umber or burnt sienna artist's oil paints to tone down paint colors that are too bright. For this cabinet project, I experimented a lot on scraps of pine board to make sure I could achieve just the right color effect on these cupboards. In this case, I found that fruitwood-colored stain (made by Zar) applied over the base paint produced just the right soft antiqued tone.

The cabinets turned out gorgeous — every bit as attractive as the high-priced line! Because of the construction of the cabinet doors, I couldn't use the European adjustable hinges so we used the face-mounted style hinges instead. First I tried polished brass, but the tone was too prominent in relation to the tone of the cabients, but then I discovered that antiqued brass looked very attractive. I used simple wooden knobs for drawer fronts.

Instructions for Creating Distressed-Look Cabinets
1. Sand the outer cabinet surfaces with fine sandpaper.
2. Seal all knots in the wood with knot sealer.
3. Apply a coat of your selected paint color. Allow to dry overnight.
4. Sand painted surface lightly with 180 grit sandpaper and then apply a second coat of paint.

5. Apply stain over painted surfaces with a rag, being careful to rub only in one direction.

6. When stain has dried, sand cupboards in the areas where wear would naturally occur, such as around the handles and the edges. Sand down to the raw wood in these areas.

7. Apply two coats of low-sheen polyurethane to the cupboard surfaces to add durability.

FINISHING FLOORS

As I discussed in Chapter 3, wood is one of the most popular options in flooring. It is easy to clean and is quite resilient to nicks and scratches. If you have new wood flooring or have had old floors sanded to bare wood, you can do the finish work yourself.

Instructions for Finishing Wide Pine Boards

1. Lightly sand bare wood with very fine sandpaper (180–200 grit), until the grain feels smooth to the touch, like a baby's bottom. Using a hand sander is effective with pine flooring since it is a soft wood. With oak or other hardwood flooring a hand sander would be a tedious chore. In the case of furniture, start with coarser grit if you're sanding out major imperfections and work your way down to fine grit. A hand sander will do the job quickly.

2. Vacuum up sawdust.

3. Go over the entire surface with a tack rag, which you can buy at the hardware store, or make your own by spraying a clean, lint-free rag with dust mop treatment until moist. (Dust mop treatment is available at janitorial supply companies.) A tack rag picks up any remaining dust particles.

4. Stain the floor by working in sections, applying stain along the grain of each board. With wide pine boards, I usually stain three at a time. Continue until job is completed. If you take a break and come back after the stain has dried, you'll find it is extremely difficult to feather in more stain.

5. Allow floor to dry completely. If any spaces have developed because boards have shrunk slightly, go along the edges (both sides) with a Q-tip or rag moistened with stain. A small paintbrush also works well for this. Be sure to wipe off any excess from the top of the boards (you don't want dark stripes along each crevice from double staining).

6. Lightly sand with 200-grit sandpaper to smooth out raised wood grain. When any liquid, like stain, is applied to wood it makes the boards feel slightly rough — thus raising the grain.

PROBLEM SOLVER

What can you do with a concrete floor?

Problem: You have a concrete floor in your newly remodeled basement, but don't have the budget for wall-to-wall carpeting or flooring.

Solution: Paint your concrete floor in a checkerboard pattern with latex paint, and finish with three coats of polyurethane. No one will ever realize the floor is concrete!

7. Vacuum and clean with tack rag again.
8. At this point determine if the stain is dark enough. If not, repeat steps 4 through 7.
9. Apply three coats of polyurethane or whatever finish you choose. Polyurethane comes in satin and high gloss finishes.

Polyurethane (poly) is a good finish and is considered more durable than acrylic. It is also more costly. Typically, three coats of poly are applied in 24-hour increments. It takes an average temperature of 65° to 75°F overnight, without humidity, for the floor to dry. Complete curing takes a couple of weeks, but in the meantime the floor can be walked on gently.

TIPS ON PAINTING

- Paint cement basement walls to make the area look cleaner and brighter. If you have a lot of leftover light-colored paint, mix the clean paint together in a large container. Mix latex with other latex paints and oil paints with other oil paints. Stir well. This works fine for those basement walls.
- Paint sprayers work wonderfully for this type of job. It's a good idea to put paint through cheesecloth in case there is any debris. Wear a respirator and make sure there is adequate ventilation.
- When painting new wood, seal knots first with a special sealer for this purpose, or they will "bleed" through.
- After priming new wood, sand lightly with very fine-grit sandpaper for a smooth finish.
- When you're finished working for the day with oil-based paint, wrap the brush in a plastic bag, fasten securely, and put in the freezer. You won't have to clean the brush before you resume work the next day.
- Trim paint stands out more if the color is deeper. Use three times the pigment formula than that used for the walls.
- Semigloss paint for trim is washable and more durable.
- Shoe polish and shoe polish dye are terrific for small stain jobs or touch-ups.
- White shoe polish can be used to "antique" bricks that are too red. A little black polish will also add character.
- Driftwood Minwax stain can give white-painted trimwork a weathered-barn-board look. Apply it with a brush and then wipe off with a cloth. The effect will be streaked, like wood grain.
- Use burnt umber or burnt sienna artist's oil paint to fill in scratch marks on furniture or wood floors or a new oil painting. Wipe the oil paint on with a rag.
- Are some of your light fixtures the wrong color? Spray-paint them if you can remove them, or hand paint. White kitchen light fixtures that have yellowed with age are brightened up with white enamel paint; brass can be changed to wrought-iron black to fit your decor.
- Do you hate the way your brass fireplace and glass doors look? Paint them black and they won't be so noticeable. Use paint specifically formulated for metal.
- Spray guns for exterior use work well — if you use the commercial size. Smaller guns clog easily.
- Oil-based polyurethane is more durable than acrylic poly.
- When you're finished spray painting, hold the can upside down and spray until the paint no longer comes out to clean the nozzle.
- You'll save yourself a lot of trouble if you mark the paint can with a stripe of its own paint while the can is open.
- Wood tone trim in a small area makes the area look smaller. Paint the trim the same color as the walls or slightly darker for visual expansion.

The problem with poly is that if the floor is subjected to heavy traffic and a lot of grit, the surface will get worn, and the damaged surface is difficult to patch up or remove. If you anticipate a particularly high traffic area that will drag in considerable grit on the bottom of shoes, consider an alternative product to polyurethane. I have had success in this situation with a product called sanding sealer. When the floor gets scratched, I clean it well and apply another coat of sanding sealer. (I understand that this technique is not recommended by floor experts, but it has worked for me.) I had a kitchen floor that received an enormous amount of wear and tear: wood stove, children, animals, and lots of traffic in and out from the barn. The entire house had oak floors, which received three coats of poly. All the floors held up fine except in the kitchen. Within one year the floor was a mess. On my hands and knees I sanded down the floor again — a horrific job. Knowing the same problem would only occur again, I came up with the sanding sealer trick. When the surface of the kitchen floor began to show wear, I applied a coat of sanding sealer. For over ten years I continued to avoid refinishing by applying sanding sealer, and the floor looked fine.

To determine what shade your floor will be with poly or a sealer on it, using no stain, dampen your finger and rub a spot on the floor. This is how the finish will deepen the natural wood. Use this test when making the decision to stain wood or not. If the wet spot is to your liking, apply only a finish.

REFINISHING FURNITURE

When do you make the decision to strip an entire piece of furniture (or part of it) rather than simply add a new coat of paint? There are two reasons for completely stripping and refinishing a piece:

- A wood-tone look fits best into your decorating scheme.
- The exterior finish of the piece of furniture is badly damaged.

How to strip it. It may be that the piece of furniture in question is nicely painted, but it would fit much better in your decorating if it were brought back to a wood-tone finish with the grain showing through. To do this requires removing all the paint or existing finish on the piece. You can strip the piece of furniture yourself or you can have it commercially dipped in stripper solution. Stripping it yourself is kinder to the furniture than having the piece dipped. Dipping, which involves submerging the entire piece of furniture in a really strong solution, is very effective at removing multiple layers of paint, but it also weakens the glue (once they're dipped, chairs are never the same) and raises the grain of the wood. You'll need to do a lot of follow-up sanding to get a smooth grain surface on a dipped piece.

For pieces that are valuable or fairly straight-lined, or if you have time to spare, I recommend doing the stripping job yourself. Really large pieces

> ### TIPS FOR INSTALLING PINE WOOD FLOORS
>
> Before flooring is laid down, staple black roofing paper over the entire floor. That way, any spaces that develop won't be so noticeable and the felt paper acts as a cushion and helps prevent squeaks. Further, you can snap chalk lines on the paper to help keep your lines straight.
>
> Baseboards should be removed before flooring installation. In new construction, cut baseboards to size, number them, and remove to paint. After the floor is laid and stained or painted, install the baseboards.

coated with numerous layers of paint that you will never get around to doing yourself are worth having dipped. Full-sized room doors with many layers of paint are also worth having done commercially.

Set-up and materials required. Stripping is a messy job. First fine a working area that isn't going to suffer if the solvent splatters. It should also be well-ventilated because the solvent produces heavy fumes. You will need to cover the floor with several layers of newspaper or a plastic tarp. You will also need to protect yourself by wearing a long-sleeved shirt and pants, goggles, and gloves. Paint remover can burn the skin; heavy-duty gloves are a must.

You'll find a variety of brands of paint remover products. I prefer the thicker formulas have more body and can by applied with a brush. Try to position the object you're refinishing at table height to eliminate back pain as you work. It also helps make the job easier if the surface you're working on is in a horizontal position.

Removal process. Apply the paint remover with a brush to a small area of the surface your're refinishing, about a square foot at a time. Let stand for several minutes so the remover softens the finish, then use a scraper and scoop off the loose paint goop and drop it onto the newspaper on the floor. Continue this process, applying remover to one area at a time, until you have completed the whole surface. A heavily painted piece may require a couple coats of remover to make it completely clean. Once most of the original finish is removed, you will usually need to go over the piece again to remove residue using a piece of steel wool coated with remover or denatured alcohol. There are always a few places that require a little digging with a sharp object to remove all the paint, such as corners and crevices.

Sanding. After the paint is removed, you will need to sand the wood surface of your piece. The goal with sanding is to do as little as possible. The best possible scenario is to lightly sand with fine sandpaper just to smooth out the raised grain caused by the paint remover. But there will be times when ink stains, deep gouges, and such will have damaged the furniture surface so badly that the only option is to get down to bare wood. For such jobs, I use a hand-held sander over the entire piece. I start with coarse grit sandpaper, then go to medium grit and finish with fine grit. (You can purchase a package containing assorted grits of sandpaper at the hardware or lumber store.) Change the sandpaper often, especially when using the coarse grit. If you try to make the sandpaper last it will take too long to attain the required smoothness. After you've used a sander for a little while, you'll get the feel of the smoothness desired.

How much to sand. The decision about how much to sand really comes down to personal taste. Some people want their furniture to have a highly polished, no mars, perfect finish. Others like the feel of worn, lived-with, well-used pieces. The less done to change the original patina of the wood, the more valuable the piece is likely to be in the antiques world. It is very common to find furniture on which, after many years, the shellac or varnish has become very dark. Removing the finish will usually reveal a lovely tone of wood that requires only light sanding before a finish can be applied. If you discover any original painted design in the process of stripping an old piece, ask someone knowledgeable in the field before removing it. You might possibly have a valuable piece.

Selecting a stain color. One a piece of furniture is stripped to the bare wood, you have the choice of which wood-tone stain to apply. This may be determined by the placement of the piece in your home decor. If the furniture in the family room is all shades of cherry and the piece is to go there, then you'll want to use a tone that blends with those. But, as with wood floors, the choice is personal. Just because the tone of a particular wood is typical doesn't mean it has to be. Oak can be stained walnut, pine can be stained cherry, cherry can be stained mahogany, and so on.

Applying stain. Stain is usually applied with a rag. Many pieces will require two coats of stain to get the desired effect. Allow at least 24 hours of drying time between coats and before a finish coat is applied.

Finishes. There are many types of finishes available for wood-stained pieces; the most popular is polyurethane (poly). Poly comes in a variety of gloss finishes, from low luster to a high gloss. You can achieve a nice finish by applying two or three coats of poly, sanding lightly in between coats.

For finishing antique furniture, a mixture of one part linseed oil to two parts turpentine is my favorite standby. When you first apply this mixture to the piece with a rag, you'll find that the wood just slurps it up. Continue to apply the mixture regularly over several months and you'll find that the wood will gradually begin to take longer to dry. Once this happens, you can apply the mixture less frequently. After several years of using this finish on furniture, a beautiful low-gloss patina develops.

There are also gel-form products available that combine stain color with finish. These are easy to use and work well for certain applications. I used a brick-red gel over a light oak vanity and was thrilled with the result. No further finish was necessary as the poly was combined with the color.

Choosing a finish requires a bit of trial and error. Read the labels on the products available, select one that sounds like what you're looking for, then do a test patch in an inconspicuous spot on your piece of furniture. If you're not satisfied, try another product. Paint store salespeople can be extremely helpful in telling you what products sell best and explaining how to use them. They sell to the "trade painters" and are often willing to share the knowledge they've acquired from the professionals.

Tiling Projects

Ceramic tile is one of the oldest and most durable surfacing materials. Tiles have been found in the ruins of ancient Eygptian and Roman homes and baths. After many centuries, the tiles remain intact on temples, cathedrals, and palaces. There are literally thousands of choices of tile available. Prices run the range from very reasonable to expensive. The more decorative they are, generally the more costly. They come in a beautiful range of colors and designs that fit into any decor. Tile will enhance your home's appearance and value. It's a good do-it-yourself project, well worth trying.

TOOLS

Tiling requires just a few tools. The only expensive tool is a wet saw, which is a circular saw with a diamond-edge blade that is designed to be used with water to keep it cool and help keep the dust down. It can cut tile or brick facing and score whole bricks. A fairly decent wet saw can cost $600 and up, so unless you're planning to do a lot of tiling, it would be wiser to rent one.

Another option is to have the tile cut at the store where you purchase it. This is economical only if you don't have too many cuts to make. First install all the whole tiles, then mark the ones needing cuts and take them to the store. The fee per tile is nominal, but numerous cuts could end up being quite costly. So be sure to check on the price before buying the tile. (Note: Even if you have rented a tile cutter, it is sometimes more expeditious to have the tough cuts — e.g., holes for outlets in the middle of a tile — done by an experienced person.)

Besides a wet saw, you will need:

- Nippers to cut the tile in curves where required
- Laundry marker for marking cuts on tiles (regular ink is water-soluble)
- Metal trowel with different-sized teeth for thin set
- Rubber trowel for grouting (also called a float)
- Putty knife
- Rags
- Container for mixing grout (a gallon-sized plastic milk container, rinsed and cut down)
- Rubber gloves
- Thin set and latex additive (admix) to make the adhesive easier to spread, reduce shrinkage, and increase the bonding capacity

TECHNIQUE

Tiling has some tricky aspects to it but is not hard to do. The tricky parts take practice and perseverance.

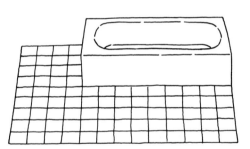

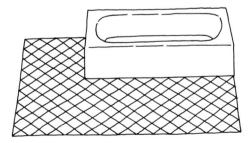

Tile can be laid out in a standard pattern (above) or on the diagonal (below), which requires more intricate cutting.

Cutting the tile. For this job you need an appropriate-sized wet saw. If you are using 12″ tile, rent a saw for 12″ tile. A saw sized for 8″ tile will slow the job and waste a lot of tile and time for the amateur. Tile laid on the diagonal requires many more intricate cuts than tile laid out in a regular pattern, but it is a very effective way to lay a floor.

Laying out the tile. Do a dry run first and check the layout carefully before making it permanent. Be sure the tiles are evenly spaced, that row lines follow all the way through, and that no tiny pieces of tile are required on the ends.

Tiling is one of those jobs that work better with two people: one person to make the tile cuts and the other to mix the grout and lay the tiles.

Step-by-Step Instructions for Tiling

1. **Set up the wet saw on a worktable.** The saw is mounted in a large tray approximately 16″x 24″x 3½″ deep. Fill the tray with several inches of clean water. To protect the floors and walls from the spray produced when the saw is operating, cover the area well with a 10′x12′ plastic tarp.

2. **Prepare the surface.** The surface to be tiled should be extremely rigid and strong. Cement board and ⅝″ plywood are most often used for countertops. If ceramic tiling is to be installed on a floor, two layers of ⅝″ plywood fastened down with screws are recommended. (You should be able to jump on the floor and feel absolutely no vibration.)

3. **Prepare the thin set.** Thin set is one type of product that can be used to fasten the tile to a base. A liquid latex additive is recommended for preventing powdering and cracking. To mix the thin set, first put two to three cups of powdered mixture in a container. (You can always make more.) Stir in the latex additive gradually until the mixture looks like cake batter with no lumps. Let the mixture rest for ten minutes. *Note:* Thin set powder comes in at least two different colors, white and gray. If you are planning to use white or very light-colored grout, use the white thin set so that any particles that aren't covered in the grout line won't be noticeable.

4. **Apply the thin set.** With a trowel apply thin set to the surface to be tiled and spread it with the serrated edge. Then apply thin set to each tile by "buttering" it on the wrong side and finishing with the serrated edge.

5. **Lay the tile.** Put each tile in place and apply a little pressure. For a kitchen counter, lay the tile for the countertop first and then do the backsplash area. Using a rubber mallet and a 2x4 board, move the board across the tiles gradually to check level, gently tapping any spot that seems to be slightly raised.

Spread thin set on prepared surface with serrated-edged trowel.

Use plastic spacers to lay tiles evenly.

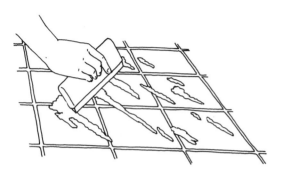

Spread the grout over the tiles, filling all the crevices evenly, using a rubber-backed trowel.

Many tiles have built-in spacers attached — small edges that provide space for the grout line. If your tiles don't have spacers attached, buy them separately. These tiny plastic crosses, placed at the intersection of four tiles, ensure that you leave room for grout. They come in different sizes; your tile store clerk will suggest the appropriate size.

6. **Prepare and apply the grout.** After all the tiles are down, grouting is the finishing step. The tile store clerk can tell you how much grout you need for the amount of tile you purchased. Allow tiles to dry overnight before grouting. Don't mix all the grout at once unless you're working on a very small area — less than 10 square feet. Add latex additive to the grout powder until the mixture resembles cake batter. Let stand about 10 minutes.

Spread the grout between the tiles with a rubber-backed trowel (float), making sure all crevices are filled evenly. Bring the float across the countertop at an angle. After the grout has set for 10 to 15 minutes, wipe off the excess and clean up the area with a clean, damp cloth. For additional information on tile installation, see the books listed in the reading list on page 127.

Sources

Most of the materials mentioned in this book can be easily found at your local lumber store, home decorating supply store, or fabric store. There are a few products, however, that I have used and found to be outstanding in meeting a particular need. Some of these are not easy to find, so I have listed the suppliers here. You might first ask your local supplier if they stock or can special-order the product.

HIDEAWAY SCREEN "DOORS"

This screen is on a roller so that when not in use the screens retract and are encased in a cassette that is barely noticeable along the door frame. I particularly wanted this type of screen for the French door units in my dining room area. The company, called Genius Superior Screens, makes both vertical and horizontal models in a variety of sizes. I used a vertical style on my door; These screen doors are terrific for anyone who finds the dimming effects of large patio screen doors a distraction. This type of screen is also perfect for a front door that you occasionally want to be able to leave open without bugs getting in.

Available from: Screenex Division, 759 Zena Highwood Road, Kingston (Woodstock), NY 12401. 914/246-3432.

PERIOD LIGHTING

Wonderful handmade reproductions of early American lighting. Country Traditions is the name of their more moderately priced line.

Available from: Period Lighting, River Road, Clarksburg, MA 01247. 413/664-7141.

CARADEO WOOD WINDOWS

Caradeo makes thermopane simulated divided-light windows which are half the cost of true divided-light windows. This is a nice product.
Available from: Caradeo, 201 Evans Road, Rantoul, IL 61866. 217/893-4444.

ZAR WOOD STAIN

This is a stain and sealer combination and one coat is all you need to achieve the desired tone. It comes in a wide variety of color choices. A coat of polyurethane or some other finishing product is required for durability.
Available from: United Gilsonite Laboratories, Scranton, PA 18501.

WALL COVERINGS

For a textured wallpaper look, I recommend the textured wallpaper brand Applique, manufactured by Imperial Wallcoverings of Cleveland. It is available in hardware stores.

High-relief embossed wall coverings (by the brand names Lincrusta and Anaglypta) are available. You can apply a variety of finishes to resemble more expensive coverings such as oak paneling, carved wood, plaster work, metal work, or cordovan leather. These coverings are available from: Crown Corporation, 1801 West Van Koap Street, Suite 235, Denver, CO 80202. 303/292-1313. Product brochure available.

FLOORING

Kahrs International, 951 Mariners Island, Suite 630, San Mateo, CA 94404.

Further Reading

Colonial Homes Magazine. Red Oak, IA. 800/888-1616.

Coyle, Carolyn. *Designing with Tile.* New York: Van Nostrand Reinhold, 1995.

Dorey, Sasha. *Decorative Stamping: Hundreds of Projects for Your Home.* Pownal, VT: Storey Publishing, 1996.

Falcone, Joseph D. A.I.A. *How to Design, Build, Remodel and Maintain Your Home.* New York: Fireside Edition, Simon & Schuster, Inc., 1995.

The Home Workshop. Alexandria, VA: Time-Life, Inc., 1990.

Luke, Heather. *Design and Make Curtains and Drapes.* Pownal, VT: Storey Communications, 1996.

————.*Design and Make Fabric Window Shades.* Pownal, VT: Storey Communications, 1996.

Reenen, Lani van. *Make Your Own Curtains & Blinds.* Pownal, VT: Storey Communications, 1994.

————.*Make Your Own Cushions & Covers.* Pownal, VT: Storey Communications, 1994.

Sloan, Annie, and Kate Gwynn. *Color in Decoration.* New York, NY: Little Brown & Co., 1990.

Sprigg, June, and David Larkin. *Shaker: Life, Work, & Art.* Boston, MA: Houghton Mifflin Co., 1987.

Waring, Janet. *Early American Stencils on Walls & Furniture.* New York, NY: Dover Publications, 1937.

Index